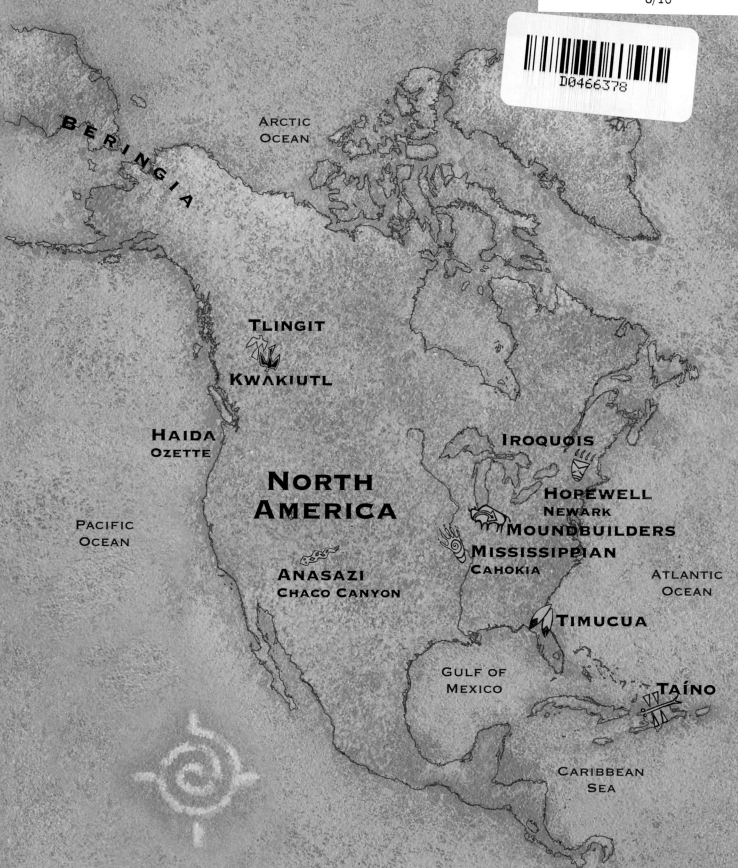

BERINGIA

ARCTIC
OCEAN

TLINGIT

KWAKIUTL

HAIDA
OZETTE

PACIFIC
OCEAN

NORTH
AMERICA

ANASAZI
CHACO CANYON

IROQUOIS

HOPEWELL
NEWARK
MOUNDBUILDERS
MISSISSIPPIAN
CAHOKIA

ATLANTIC
OCEAN

TIMUCUA

GULF OF
MEXICO

TAÍNO

CARIBBEAN
SEA

The First

AMERICANS

The Story of Where They Came From and Who They Became

ANTHONY AVENI

Illustrations by S. D. Nelson

SCHOLASTIC NONFICTION

An Imprint of

SCHOLASTIC

ACKNOWLEDGMENTS

Thank you to Kate Waters, Elysa Jacobs, Brenda Murray, Nancy Sabato, Tatiana Sperhacke, Dwayne Howard, Lorraine Aveni, Jordan Kerber, Sean Janney and his mom, Diane, and Augie Nanz and his mom, Cathy, for helping me to tell my story.

LIBRARY OF CONGRESS CATALOGING-IN-PUBLICATION DATA
Aveni, Anthony F.
The First Americans: The Story of Where They Came From and Who They Became / by Anthony Aveni
Includes bibliographical references and index.
1. Indians—Migrations.   2. Indians—Origin.   3. Human beings—Bering Land Bridge—Migrations.   4. Indians of North America—History.
I. Title.
E59.M58A94 2005
970.01—dc22   2004041667

ISBN 0-439-55144-7

10 9 8 7 6 5 4 3 2   05 06 07 08 09

Printed in Singapore   46
First printing, October 2005

Contents

A Journey Across Two Continents

How long could you last without TV, your computer, or your bike? How about doing without heating and air-conditioning, cars, and microwaves? Technology is so important to us that it's no wonder so many people believe that high-tech aliens built the huge pyramids and intricately carved monuments that are the evidence of ancient cultures on our continent.

In fact, America was discovered by earth people, and in *The First Americans: The Story of Where They Came From and Who They Became*, we are going to discover them.

For migrating people, getting food from the land meant every member of the family needed to help—including kids.

We begin not in 1492, but when the peopling of America first began—about 20,000 years ago, in the far north of Alaska where a land bridge once connected North America to Asia. Asian migrants were forced to follow the game they hunted across that bridge. In several waves of migration, they crossed Canada into the United States. Eventually they trickled down into South America as their descendants evolved over hundreds and hundreds of generations to become the different cultural groups we call American Indians. These migrants mixed bloods, genes, languages, and customs. They left behind remains of pots, bones, tools, weapons, and rock carvings for the archaeologists and historians who would piece together their past.

Once the climate changed and the land bridge disappeared beneath the ocean waves, the first North Americans were here to stay. And what a diverse group of cultures they would become—Haida, Mississippian, Hopewell, Anasazi, and Taíno! Though many of their descendants would die of smallpox and other diseases brought over by the Europeans, the survivors would gradually mix with the English, Spanish, and French who entered our continent from the east thousands of years after the first migrations. That mixing is part of what gives the Americas their unique populations today.

How do we know? We'll begin by piecing together in Chapters 1 and 2 the evidence that tells about the first migration and the first contact of the migrants' descendants with the Europeans.

We'll try to imagine the hardships of the long, endless waves of migration that lasted for many generations. And we'll wonder how strange it must have been for Taíno descendants of the migrants to confront Columbus thousands of years later on the shores of a tiny island in the Caribbean—as strange as it might be for you to meet up with an alien from space!

Then, in Chapters 3 through 7, we'll begin to fill in the thousands of years in between. We'll make journeys to five different regions of North America and study the people who lived there. Though we'll find significant differences among the natives of the Northeast, Midwest, Southwest, Northwest, and Southeast United States, we'll discover that all these people are descendants of that first migration.

We'll start with the Woodland peoples of the Northeast—the people of the longhouse. They organized a constitution that inspired the Founding

Fathers of the United States when they wrote one for the new country.

Then come the Moundbuilders from the middle of our country. They molded mysterious giant figures of octagons, circles, serpents, and birds out of the land. You can still see some of these figures today in Ohio.

We'll travel to the Southwest to meet the ancient Anasazi. They lived in huge apartment complexes long before we did.

Our next stop will be the Northwest Coast, where native people took gift-giving to the extreme. They gave away their most precious possessions, hoping that in return they would receive even bigger gifts from rival clans.

We'll journey to the Southeast to experience a day in the life of the Timucua. These exotic people invented barbecue, and they hunted alligators using only their bare hands and sticks.

Chapter 8 is about America's first great city—a city that thrived long before our modern cities of New York, Miami, Denver, and Seattle were built. Unlike our cities, those of the first Americans were all built by the descendants of people who came here in the great migrations. We'll go to Cahokia (kuh-**hoh**-kee-uh), near St. Louis, where the Mississippi and Missouri Rivers join. We call Cahokia a city because so many people lived there. These people created things that impress us today—big monuments, great architecture, and beautiful pottery and sculpture. We think of these city people as more advanced and more organized than people who lived simple lives in small villages. But what all cities have in common is that they each develop a great tradition that is maintained over a long time—a way of living that affects, and even transforms, many of the cultures their people came in contact with. We will try to understand what makes up the great tradition of Cahokia as we join archaeologists on a dig that will take us down below the earth's surface and into the past of this great city. We'll discover its courts and temples, streets and fortifications, and the remains of the art, jewelry, burial practices, and tools of the people who built it.

As we dig the legacy of the first North Americans out of our soil, we'll find people who seem different from us. We'll wonder why they focused so much attention on clans and groups of people and so little on the individual, the way we do. And why did they pay so much attention to their dead—as much attention as our culture gives to sports?

This is what archaeologists think Cahokia looked like around 1000 BCE when it was the biggest city in North America.

To answer these questions, we'll need to probe their lifestyles. We'll explore why sacrifice was so important to them and why their children needed to be responsible members of society at a very early age.

In the last chapter, we'll focus on some basic questions about how archaeologists, forensic experts, and people who study native languages discover the truth about the first people who lived in our land.

Why study the first Americans? For the same reason we study any people who have inhabited our planet before us—to learn from them by understanding where they succeeded and why they failed. That's the lesson of history.

The Great Migration

It is 20,000 years ago in Beringia—a frigid land now submerged in a shallow sea that lies between Alaska and Siberia. You stand on the edge of a high cliff surrounded by glaciers that gleam in the bright sunlight. The ground is wet with a layer of melting springtime snow. You can see your breath. Stretched out on either side of you in a long line are your mother, your father, several aunts and uncles, and your cousins—about a hundred family members in all. Most of you hold small spears. Your father cradles an atlatl (a-tul-a-tul), and one of your uncles twirls a sling. Others have lighted torches.

This cave painting proves that wearing a disguise is a very old custom. But what could it have to do with hunting deer?

You speak in whispers as your gaze follows a mile-long line of caribou meandering in the grassy valley below. What happens in the next hour will determine whether your family will survive. All of you depend on the meat, the blood, and the fat of the caribou for food. Their hides will become your clothing, their muscles your thread, and their bones your needles and scrapers.

Antlers from a previous hunt make up the headdresses you wear—not just to disguise yourselves, but to make magic. Last night, by the light of the moon, your mother's sister made drawings of this spring's caribou hunt on the wall of the cave. She chanted to the ancestor gods: "Let this be true—that our family will survive the long trip our ancestors began many, many years ago to this prosperous new land." Your family tribe is on the edge of starvation. The remains of the 14-foot-tall (as tall as a giraffe) mastodon you killed last fall, along with the stored supply of dried roots and berries, are practically all gone. But your mother's oldest brother, the head of the clan, assured you a few days ago at the campfire that the herd will soon come this way. The caribou begin to migrate eastward every year when the stars of Orion disappear and the Big Dipper rises high in the morning sky.

It has been a very long winter. You reflect on how busy you and your brothers and sisters have been for the last three full moons, helping to prepare for the early spring hunt and the migration that will follow. Eventually you'll settle in at another encampment farther to the east and south.

As you wait and watch, you remember stories of last year's hunt. One member of the clan was stomped by a mammoth. Your uncle got a foot-long scar on his upper thigh where he was jabbed by a long tusk. His younger brother encountered a saber-toothed tiger. Your heart is pounding anxiously in your chest as you stand poised for action on the ridge.

Then, just as the midline of the caribou herd passes below you, the wise leader of your family tribe, the one who wears the largest antlers, gives the signal—a loud shriek: *O—o—o—o—eee!* Everyone breaks into a shout and bounds down the cliffside, setting fire to the grass as they go. Stampede! The

DANGEROUS ENCOUNTERS!

It must have been like living in a zoo! Lions, bears (bigger than the ones we know), and reindeer (caribou) seem familiar enough, but if you were trekking across ancient North America 10,000 years ago, you would likely also run into now-extinct animals like the unpredictable woolly mammoth, the fierce saber-toothed tiger, and the 6,000-pound, 20-foot-long giant ground sloth. (Don't worry, it's a harmless vegetarian.)

Archaeologists excavated this spear point next to a buffalo's ribs, remains of a 10,000-year-old hunt in New Mexico (top). The saber-toothed tiger (bottom) gets its name from those long canines.

The advantage of the atlatl is that it extends your arm—which means you can throw your spear faster and farther.

startled herd bolts forward. Even the fastest runners can't keep up with the fleet-footed caribou, which can gallop up to 30 miles per hour. But because the ambush is spread out along the line of the flank, you can direct the caribou run into a narrow gully with a steep wall on the opposite side.

The caribou begin to bunch up as the gully narrows. Success! The plan is working! One animal manages to jump out of the trap, but another falls back and tumbles into the forelegs of its nearest companion. As both of them topple, several more caribou stumble helplessly into the traffic jam. Meanwhile, your dad takes aim with the atlatl. He lifts it over his shoulder and, with a whiplike action, hurtles the spear with lethal force toward a running target 150 feet away—strike! As you catch up to the back of the confused herd, you can see the terror in their eyes. You can smell their sweat. You charge ahead and take aim at a fleeing cow. But you release your spear too early and it glances harmlessly off a boulder. Dejected, you turn away, only to catch sight of your little brother, who has begun to descend into the gully to pursue a

stray calf. You rush forward and barely manage to pull him out of the path of a charging bull farther down the line. Other spears hit home, and though most of the animals escape, within an hour dozens of caribou lie dead, piled on top of one another in a long line down the gully.

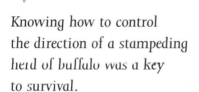

Knowing how to control the direction of a stampeding herd of buffalo was a key to survival.

Like most successful hunts, this one is an overkill. You have killed more animals than you can eat—even over an entire winter. You know it's wasteful, and perhaps someday the caribou, like the mammoths, will become scarce, but there is little else you can do. When your hunting strategy works and your life depends on it, you must follow the time-tested plan. Now the hard work begins. You must skin and prepare the hides, and cut chunks of meat into strips to dry over the fire. You will eat the most perishable parts first—highly prized organs like the liver, which you will eat raw. Your uncle will divide it up and give a small piece to everyone as he thanks the ancestor gods for giving your family life for another year. Your mom will use the lungs, the stomach, and the heart, together with wild onions and roots, to make a stew. Once

you have scraped the flesh from the hides, your older sister will dry them over the fire, trim them, and comb them out. But you must work fast. You have only about two weeks until the thin crescent moon reappears in the west. That's the signal to begin the seasonal trek eastward and southward, as you follow the route of the animals into a vast, new, and unexplored land. The sun god will remain in the sky for most of the day in the coming months to guide you.

This human-made tool kit contains scrapers for cleaning hides (6), a spokeshave for shaping spear shafts (2), grovers for boring holes to make needles out of bones (3 and 7), a spear point (8), and several knives (1, 4, and 5).

You and your family will be on the move for the rest of your lives as you advance farther along the route your ancestors have taken every spring and summer in search of game. People will come after you, year after year, in waves of migration, until Beringia sinks beneath the waves of melting glaciers. Eventually your descendants will populate all of North and South America from Alaska to Tierra del Fuego. You will fill these continents with people thousands of years before Columbus even dreams of coming to the New World. And all the while, none of you will ever know that you were making history!

HOW TO NAVIGATE AND TELL THE TIME BY THE STARS

Big Dipper   Milky Way   Orion

Little Dipper

Vega   Polaris

Archaeologists doubt the ancient Beringians had star maps like this one used by the Pawnee in the nineteenth century, but by memorizing star patterns and following star movements, ancient people found their way over vast distances.

Today, the North Star, also called Polaris, which lies at the end of the Little Dipper constellation, marks the location of the pole about which all the stars rotate. Pawnee descendants of the ancient Beringians call it "the star that does not move." But at the time of the great migration, the bright star Vega was close to this fixed point in the sky. It would have served as a very bright beacon to help hunter-gatherers find their way around an unfamiliar environment.

If we didn't have watches and calendars, we'd probably still be telling time by the stars. Anyone who goes out and looks at the night sky is familiar with the summer Milky Way and the winter appearance of Orion the Hunter and his faithful dogs Canis Major and Canis Minor. By repeatedly watching the sky, ancient Beringians knew that when the stars of the Orion constellation disappeared over the western horizon in early morning twilight, the snow would begin to melt. This was a signal for them to prepare for the hunt.

This Pawnee star chart, painted on buckskin, marks the stars still sacred to these people, including the Big and Little Dippers, Vega, and the brilliant stars in Orion.

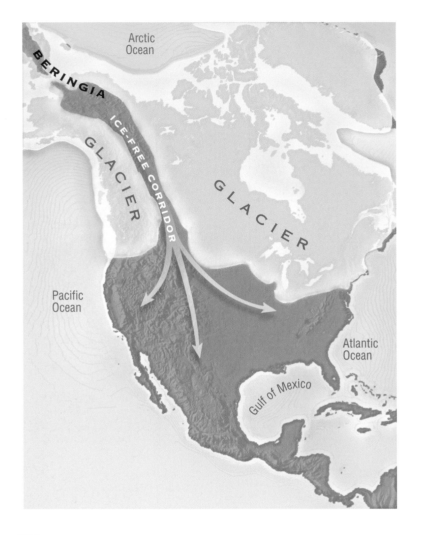

Arctic
Ocean

BERINGIA

ICE-FREE CORRIDOR

GLACIER

GLACIER

Pacific
Ocean

Atlantic
Ocean

Gulf of Mexico

The ancient Beringians came from *Asia* in waves by several routes and throughout many generations to eventually populate all of the Americas.

It is the mid-1970s. Archaeologists from the University of Pittsburgh probe a rockfall at Meadowcroft, a cavernous rock shelter by the side of a creek in western Pennsylvania. Over the years, local residents have reported finding flint arrowheads there. The archaeologists learn that, on a number of occasions, rocks have broken loose and fallen to the cave floor, protecting the remains that lie buried there. All together they will excavate eleven layers, down to a depth of 11½ feet. Out of these undisturbed layers they will eventually pull more than 3½ million ancient artifacts, including the bones of more than 100 different animal species. From one layer alone, they will catalog 400 stone artifacts. Not all of them are made from local stone, which means that whoever visited Meadowcroft probably came from far away. The archaeologists will also discover a fire pit with pieces of charcoal as well as charred remains of the world's oldest basket, which is made out of bark. They will use these materials to date that layer. (Radiocarbon dating is explained on page 114.)

We know that Meadowcroft was occupied off and on for more than 5,000 years by descendants of the ancient Beringians who built on top of one

We all carry with us the things we need to survive: money, a wallet, keys to the house, and maybe a lucky charm. The artifacts recovered along the migration route by archaeologists tell us a lot about the lifestyles of the earliest descendants of the Beringians who inhabited our continent. What did these first Americans carry? Scrapers made of bone for cleaning hides, sharp flint knives to cut through big bones, and many tools.

The rounded points found all over North America are called Clovis points, after the site in New Mexico where they were first discovered. The dates of the sites where Clovis points have been found coincide with the last breakup of the glaciers. That's about 3,000 years ago, about the time mastodons were totally hunted out of existence. But more recently, sites 10,000 years older than that have been found. One of them, Monte Verde, lies near the coast of Chile in South America. There, archaeologists have excavated remains of huts, charcoal pits, and even bones from butchered mastodons—but no Clovis points! This discovery leads archaeologists to wonder whether these trekkers moved by a separate route along the coast in the middle of the last ice age.

Can you see the places where pieces of flint were chipped away to make these spear points? Look at the sharp edges!

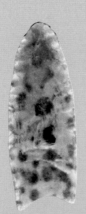

Scientists began excavating Meadowcroft, PA, in 1974. This trench runs from outside to inside the rock shelter.

another's remains. Scrapers, spear points, knives, and needles—some of the very same artifacts used by your ancestors in Beringia more than 2,000 years earlier—lie in the lowest layers. Part of the great migration that began in your ancient homeland passed through Meadowcroft. The waves of people passed through a thousand other sites in the Americas as well. It took 2,000 years. Think of it—that's enough time for eighty generations of your family to cover the 6,000 miles between Beringia and the eastern United States. It's also enough time for intermarrying and exchanging bloods and DNA with other tribes, enough time for adapting to different environments—the coast of Alaska, the Rocky Mountains, the Great Plains—even enough time for changes in the languages we speak. All the traits that once defined your ancient family have been absorbed and altered by contact with diverse people in differing environments.

Scientists from many fields of study are putting together the pieces of an exciting puzzle from clues they find in the remains you and the other trekkers have left behind—your tools, bones, even your garbage. It all points to one basic conclusion: The native tribes of North and South America—from the Eskimo to the Pawnee to the Seminoles, from the Iroquois to the Navajo to the Aztec, from the Maya to the Inca to the Amazonians—all descended from those of you who crossed the land bridge from Asia to discover America.

The Americas were among the last continents on earth to be populated. We have learned that their discovery is the story of a great migration that started at least 12,000 to 30,000 years ago. (To find out how we know, see Chapter 9.) The migration began when the glaciers started to retreat, leaving a passable land bridge between Siberia and Alaska. Small groups of people came out of Asia. They mixed and moved on as they followed the route of the animals they needed to live near. These hunter-gatherers tried hard to adapt to the windy, bitterly cold climate of Beringia. Before the land bridge connecting Asia and the Americas was inundated by the rising sea, thousands of small tribes fanned out across North America.

It would take hundreds of centuries and many waves of migration before the descendants of these brave travelers would become the Hopewell, who would erect Ohio's great earthen mounds; the Hopi and the Navajo, today's relatives of the ancient Anasazi, who would inhabit Chaco Canyon, New Mexico, and Mesa Verde, Colorado; and the Caribbean Taíno, the first people to lay eyes on a ship coming from the east to "discover the New World." The year was 1492. The "discoverer" was Christopher Columbus. Wouldn't he have been amazed to learn of the true history of the discovery of America that we have just explored?

2 • FIRST CONTACT

The Taíno

So that they might be very friendly toward us . . . I gave to one of them red caps and glass beads which they hung on their necks, and many other things of little value. . . . Later, they came swimming to the ship's boats where we were. They brought to us: parrots, balls of cotton thread, [wooden] spears, and many other things. . . . Some [Indians] paint themselves a blackish color. . . . Some paint themselves white, some red. . . . They are generally of good stature, fine appearances and well built. . . . They ought to be good servants . . . [and] would easily become Christians, because it seemed to me they belonged to no creed.

—Friday, October 12, 1492

Insula hyspana

This early colonial drawing (1493) shows Columbus's ship docked on Hispaniola while the first explorers exchange gifts with the Taíno.

These words are from Christopher Columbus's journal. He wrote them about the first meeting of Europeans and Americans—a dramatic and sudden contact between two worlds. Columbus thought he had arrived in the islands off the east coast of Asia, where he had hoped to acquire great wealth by bringing back rare spices. That's why he called the land the "Indies" and the "painted" people who lived there "Indians"—a name that stuck. They were actually the Taíno, a Native American tribe.

Like Columbus, the Taíno also had been traveling. Though archaeologists cannot trace their descent step by step back to the ancient Beringians, we know that the Taíno actually descended from people who had migrated from the coast of South America along a chain of islands we call the Greater Antilles. They landed on the island of Hispaniola, which is shared today by the Dominican Republic and Haiti. Archaeologists have excavated stone tools dating to as early as 400 BCE (before the current epoch, or counting back from year zero) that were left there by descendants of the great migration out of Beringia. Though the original Taíno culture has vanished, the journals of Columbus and other explorers who followed him record many words that tell us about their environment and their social customs—words like *barbecue, canoe, hammock, hurricane,* and *tobacco* were passed on to our language.

There was so much Columbus didn't know about the "simple" people he discovered. They weren't uncivilized—they were just *different* from the people who made up his culture. Their farming methods were different from those of the Europeans. The Taíno were very efficient farmers who were well adapted to their environment. They grew cotton, papaya, pineapple, squash, yahutía (ya-hoo-**tee**-uh) (a kind of potato), and sweet potatoes. Cazabe, or cakes made out of cassava, were their bread. A cassava looks like a giant melon. (See if you can find one in a big supermarket.) The natives squeezed the poisonous juice out of its roots before grinding it. Then they made it into fat pancakes, which were cooked on a griddle. Cassava has a large root system that requires lots of air in the soil. So the Taíno learned to grow them in conucos (con-**oo**-cohs), huge dirt mounds as tall as a man and 10 feet wide.

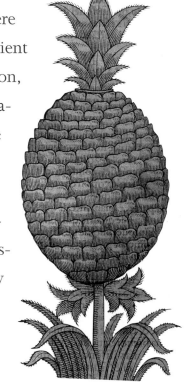

Taíno families were different from European families. They inherited their last names from their mothers instead of their fathers. If you were the king of your Taíno tribe, they would call you the cacique (kah-**see**-kay). The king who preceded you would have been your mother's oldest brother (your uncle). And your successor would be your sister's son (your nephew). Taíno people also passed down their land through their mothers. Anthropologists call this a matrilineal system. As cacique, you would probably also have had

This large, sweet-tasting fruit is yellow and juicy on the inside, and has sharp spikes on the outside—a gift from the Taíno.

What animal influenced the Taíno artist who carved this zemi?

several wives. They would have come mostly from adjacent villages. Marriage was a good way to help make political alliances with neighbors.

Their religion was different from the Roman Catholic religion practiced by Columbus. They believed in many gods, or zemis (**zem**-ees) as they called them. Their supreme zemi was Yúcahu Maórocoti. He created the world and gave people cassava. Their zemi of fertility was Attabeira (at-uh-**bay**-ruh). She made the rivers flow and the crops grow, and she helped mothers give birth to healthy children. Talented Taíno artists carved images of their gods in wood, stone, bone, and shell—images that looked beautiful to them but seemed ugly to Columbus and his followers who were not familiar with the Taíno religion. Images of zemis were sometimes made of bones or skulls of dead ancestors.

In the land of the Taíno, your ancestors were always there for you. Their magical powers helped you reach your goals. Your ancestors assisted you in special ways, especially if you carried one of their effigies, or power images, with you. An effigy is like a good luck charm or amulet. You could keep their memory alive by burying a charm in a mound or by keeping it in your house. Imagine how frightened Columbus must have been when he found decorated skulls in baskets and skeletons hanging in the communal houses!

The Taíno thought the universe was different from the one Columbus learned about when he went to school. They viewed the world as a giant tree that connected the underground layer of water with the sky, where the branches of the tree blossomed into stars. If you think about the importance of trees, worshipping them might make sense: Trees give us fuel for the winter and shade during the heat of summer. Their fruit nourishes us, and from their wood we make the houses we live in and the canoes we travel by. Birds roost in trees, woodchucks burrow underground among a tree's roots, and beavers chew off tree limbs to make dams that help create a larger supply of fish in the lake. The Taíno believed that when you die, you climb a tree to get to heaven. There you may be visited by religious leaders called shamans (**shay**-mens).

Ever try catching fish the Taíno way—with a bow and arrow? We would find a fishing rod a lot easier, but the Taíno were different!

Animals on Hispaniola were different from those living in Europe. Our Western culture associates bats with witches. And some of us still think of owls as wise birds. For the Taíno, animals that fly at night were "power forms." Hunting dogs were favorite pets—and they didn't just hunt. Because they had great night vision, they were the guardians of the dead. Have you ever watched your dog dream? It twitches, whimpers, and barks softly; sometimes you can see its eyes roll. It's probably reliving the experience of chasing that chipmunk across the lawn this morning. But if you were a Taíno watching your dog twitch around that way on the

The amulets on this page and the next are associated with animals that fly at night. They represented the shapes taken on by the souls of the Taíno's dead ancestors. What animals are they?

dirt floor of your hut, you'd know it was a sign that its soul was wandering around the universe outside of its body. Like all things that move—people, plants, volcanoes, wind, rain, and you—it has a soul.

The Taíno dressed differently from Columbus and his sailors. Columbus didn't realize there was a reason for their nakedness. The unmarried wore only a cotton belt. Married women wore skirts. Caciques wore decorated robes. Body painting was done for religious ceremonies—each color stood for a power that allied a person with a particular zemi. The feathers worn on their heads were fragments of the sky. Eagle feathers helped their spirits to soar among the gods. They wore feathers of birds that lived on the ground around their legs to keep contact with our earthly world. The Taíno didn't give any really valuable objects—like feathers and zemi amulets—to Columbus.

Even their boats were different from Columbus's. The Taíno were great sailors. Men and boys took to the sea on fishing expeditions. They rowed with their shovel-like paddles in huge, hollowed-out log boats. Here's how Columbus described them:

> They are so big that forty to forty-five men came in some of them [to meet Columbus's ship]. They rowed with an oar that was like a baker's peel [a large spatula for removing bread from an oven]. . . . If they capsize,

they all immediately start swimming, they set it upright, and they bail
it out with calabashes [dried shells of squash] that they carry.

It's too bad Columbus never understood why the Taíno were so different. But there was a lot more he didn't know about Native Americans. He didn't know that only 1,000 miles away, the Aztecs of Mexico and the Incas of Peru were building vast empires on the North American continent and high in the South American Andes. And he didn't know that, in the heartland of what we now call the United States, there lived more than 10 million people. They were settled in diverse communities from Florida to Alaska and from California to New England. We are about to meet some of them.

Within one hundred years of Columbus's landing, all of these people and their remains would be rediscovered by Spanish, English, and French explorers. Though most of the Taíno would be destroyed by measles, smallpox, and influenza brought over by Columbus and his sailors, many of those remaining would commit suicide when the Spaniards broke up their families and moved them to colonial plantations. But they have left clues that tell us who they were. Like all the other Native Americans we will encounter, the Taíno are really not so different from us, at least once you understand their culture and beliefs.

Woodland Peoples

In as much as the great Father has given us this year an abundant harvest . . . [and] has protected us from the ravages of the savages . . . I, your magistrate, do proclaim that all ye Pilgrims, with your wives and little ones, do gather at ye meeting house . . . on Thursday, November 29, and render thanksgiving to ye almighty god for his blessings.

This was the proclamation for America's first Thanksgiving. It was written in 1621 in Massachusetts by Governor William Bradford, who had just led the Pilgrims through their first hard winter in a new land.

Long before the Pilgrims arrived in the New World, Native Americans who settled in the Northeast had Thanksgiving proclamations of their own, like this one:

> Great Spirit . . . we thank thee for thy goodness in causing our mother, the earth, again to bring forth her fruits. We thank thee that thou has caused Our Supporters to yield abundantly.

That proclamation—a prayer to the gods, really—was spoken by the chief of the Seneca (**sen**-uh-kuh) tribe at the start of the Green Corn festival, when they harvested the first corn crop of the season. The Seneca of upstate New York is one of more than fifty tribal groups that lived in the northeastern part of our country. Half a million men, women, and children lived in this area of North America when the British and French first started settling there in the early seventeenth century. Archaeologists call them the Woodland peoples, partly because the area they inhabited from the Great Lakes to the Atlantic Coast was then mostly covered by a thick forest. Woodlanders also had common cultural traits. Like all eastern descendants of the ancient Beringians, they spoke some form of the Algonkian language and made simple, undecorated pottery out of clay as early as 1500 BCE. By 1000 BCE, they had managed to build small villages and clear land out of the thick forest to grow corn and tobacco. They built movable fishing camps along the riverbanks, and they created pathways for hunting.

You had to be very adaptable and very clever to survive in the place we call New England. Life in the woods was harsh, with cold snowy winters and hot steamy summers. In the north country of Maine, for example, the Penobscot learned to attract moose to their hunting area by blowing a moose call—a reed instrument like a clarinet or flute made out of birch bark. They figured out how to build a snare to trap moose. The snare would be set off by the weight of the moose. The ropes would get tangled in its antlers so that the hunter could finish it off with an arrow. To make it easier to run down their prey in winter, they devised snowshoes.

Boys learned to hunt deer from their fathers and older brothers. Before Columbus, they used only the bow and arrow—and snowshoes in winter. This photograph of Chippewa Indians was taken in Minnesota in 1870.

Of all the native Woodlanders the early European settlers encountered, the Iroquois (**ee**-roh-kwoi), who migrated from Canada and lived along both shores of the eastern Great Lakes, were probably the most unusual. English explorers of the Mohawk Valley in New York State called them the Kinsmen of the Wolf because they were such fierce fighters. The Iroquois are also known as the Romans of the New World because of the sophisticated way they organized their society. About 300 years before the arrival of the Europeans, the Iroquois brought together a band of warring tribes. They created the Five Nation Confederacy, or League of the Iroquois—a sort of "United States of Indians." Each tribe of the confederacy had its own territory created by dividing the land between the lakes and the mountains into five long strips, and each had its own tribal council and chief.

The Iroquois thought of their confederacy as a great longhouse in which they all lived together. The eastern door of the longhouse was guarded by the Mohawk. It faced the great open valley of the Hudson River. The Seneca

guarded the western doorway. It overlooked the land that opened toward the Great Plains, the place where the big game roamed. In the middle lay the territory of the Oneida (oh-**nie**-duh), the Cayuga (kay-**oo**-guh), and the Onondaga (ahn-un-**dah**-guh). The Iroquois nation occupied an ideal spot from which to control the vast area of trade that covered all of the northeast. It really *was* a 200-mile-long longhouse!

Iroquois people lived in long-houses. Each person belonged to a clan. Clans are extended families in which all the members are blood-related. What made them unique is that all clan members were descended from a common female ancestor. That's why the most important person in any longhouse was the oldest woman. She was the mother of the house. When she died, the next oldest woman took over. When a man married, he took only his weapons and the clothes on his back and went to live in his wife's longhouse. Marriage within clans was strictly forbidden.

The Iroquois confederacy had other clan house rules that might

Settling in an Indian village meant building permanent residences, planting crops, and providing a central gathering place.

LIFE IN A LONGHOUSE

The Iroquois located most of their settlements on hilltops at the branching point between two rivers. That gave them safety as well as easy access to food and travel. A typical Iroquois village would be made up of six or eight longhouses surrounded by a sharp-pointed picket fence to keep out intruders.

Before modern skyscrapers, the record for the largest building in America would have gone to the Iroquois longhouse. These two-story structures were *really* long—about 100 feet, or roughly a third the length of a soccer field!—and more than 20 feet wide. They had round, sloping roofs so the snow could slide off easily. Vent holes in the roofs let out the smoke from the fire pits that were evenly spaced on the floor. Families lived in two-story compartments. Mom, Dad, and kids all slept under piles of warm fur on the ground floor. They stored their belongings—pots and pans, baskets, bows and arrows, snowshoes, cradleboards, and toys—on the second floor.

Living in a longhouse meant you'd spend most of your time in a community of uncles, aunts, and cousins. Most of your daytime activity would take place in the open corridor that ran the length of the house. About every twenty years, clans abandoned their longhouses and moved, most often because the farmland around them became overused.

Before the Dutch settlers came, longhouses like these were once the largest buildings on the island of Manhattan.

seem strange to us. For example, if a man was killed in war, his wife could demand an enemy captive, even if it meant starting a war to get one. When the captive was brought back to the longhouse, she got to decide what to do with him. She could torture and kill him—or even adopt him!

We think of honesty, fairness, and kindness to others among the virtues we admire—the characteristics that make us good citizens. The major Iroquois virtues were loyalty to the clan and bravery. If you wanted to be a strong male warrior, you needed to know how to wield weapons like the tomahawk, a hard wood club with a heavy ball on the end. You also needed to be able to endure punishment silently should the enemy capture you. You might be poked with red-hot sticks, have smoldering cords tied around your waist, get your nails pulled out, or have your hair torn off. Only then *might* you become an adopted captive, which meant you would not be harmed further and would be accepted into the tribe.

Why was there no greater Indian loyalty than to the clan? What was it that made the clan such a strong social unit? First, women controlled the clan house so that men could devote all their attention to hunting and warfare. War expeditions kept the men away from home for very long periods. That's why the women and older children also did all the planting and harvesting and caring for the smaller children in addition to governing the longhouse. Everyone had a role to play in making the clan strong—even kids.

Iroquois boys had a much more carefree life than did the girls. By the time boys were eight years old, they were expected to wander off into the woods with their friends to learn how to live off the land. They would gather fruits and roots. They would learn to shoot their arrows straight by practicing on a bear's paw nailed to a tree, then on a moving target—like a bird, a

FUN AND GAMES

Indian kids had fun, too. Lacrosse is probably the most famous sport we inherited from American Indians. Tribes from Canada to the Southeast all played the game. Lacrosse was played with long sticks with netting over one end. These were used to pass a skin-covered ball. As in our modern version of the game, goals were scored when the ball was put into a net on the opponent's end of the field. But unlike our game, theirs could go on for hours. That's because you had to score a certain number of points, usually twelve, to win. Their rules were looser, too. Rowdy players were allowed to kick, trip, tackle, punch, and even stomp on one another. An eyewitness to a Choctaw (**chahk**-taw) game wrote this:

"There are times when the ball gets to the ground, and such a confused mass rushing together around it . . . when the condensed mass of ball-sticks, and shins, and bloody noses is carried around different parts of the playing field. . . ."

A much safer Indian game was called snowsnakes. Players would make a 1,500-foot trough in the snow. They'd pack the sides down into a smooth, icy surface like an Olympic bobsled course. The idea was to see who could slide a 6-foot-long straight stick the farthest along the track. Sounds simple enough, but snowsnakes was a game of skill. As in bowling, you needed to throw the stick perfectly onto the track to get it to go far. How you designed your stick also mattered. It had to be polished smooth with wax or oil, weighted just right at the tip, and of course you had to throw it with great force at just the right angle to achieve maximum distance. Pity you if your stick flew out of the trough. Your opponents would then boo and heckle you by making animal sounds!

This American Indian war club, made out of hardwood and glass beads, was a lethal weapon in its time (about 1700). It was made by eastern Woodland Indians.

rabbit, or a squirrel—and finally by single-handedly killing a deer. A young warrior could also test his endurance and ability to deal with pain by bashing his head on a rock. When he was ready, he would go on the warpath alongside an elder. Iroquois girls, on the other hand, did chores and learned to work in the fields that they someday would control. At the age of twelve or thirteen, when her menstrual cycle began, an Iroquois girl would prepare herself by living alone for weeks in a hut outside the village. There she would fast and pray to her guardian spirit to have good health and—the most important blessing—to be fortunate enough to have lots of children.

Some historians tell us that our American nation could not have succeeded without George Washington. The Iroquois nation had a George Washington of its own. Hiawatha (hie-uh-**wah**-thuh), born either a Mohawk or an Onondaga, was the most famous Iroquois chief—the man who founded the League of the Iroquois. He got to his position by marrying a tribal chief's daughter but also because he had seven daughters himself. Hiawatha was a great speechmaker, a great organizer, and a very wise person. One day he had a powerful vision. He saw a great pine tree

FALSE FACE

Got a nosebleed that won't quit? Many Woodland people believed the best way to cure disease was to *become* the evil spirit that caused the disease in the first place. You would need to call a member of the False Face Society. He would come to your bed and put on a mask to imitate the nosebleed demon. He'd dance around you, yelling, reciting magical spells, and shaking his turtle-shell rattle at your nose until the evil spirit was driven out of your body. If the cure worked, you'd be asked to join the society—and you couldn't say no!

For Native Americans, putting on a mask meant actually becoming the thing you impersonated. Think of that next Halloween!

A NORTHEASTERN WOODLAND FASHION SHOW

hat Woodland people wore looked different in summer and winter—just like the difference in seasonal clothing northerners wear today. As you can see, clothing was no problem in the summertime. Men and women wore breechcloths. A breechcloth is a soft animal hide about 6 feet long and 1 foot wide. You pass it between your legs and then tuck in the front and back under your belt. The ends hang down like aprons—great spaces for decoration. They also wore deerskin tops and moccasins. They decorated their clothes with shells, feathers, and porcupine quills. Kids didn't wear anything!

But during the long winter, it was a different story. Then everybody needed leggings and robes. The moose's skin and the beaver's pelt provided these warm clothes. When Woodlanders skinned a moose or a deer for a robe, they were careful to make one long cut at the belly that included the shoulder and the forelegs. Then they could fit themselves snugly into the animal's skin. Besides, that also minimized the need for sewing.

Imagine how much time it would take you to make your own clothes. Compare the summer and winter clothing worn by Native Americans with modern-day fashion.

that reached to the top of the sky. The tree grew out of a strange kind of soil made up of three double principles: good health of mind and body; peace between individuals and groups; and righteousness in conduct and justice among people. The tree had five roots and had been planted on a bed of snow that stretched from a lake on one side to mountains on the other. Hiawatha believed that the tree was humanity and the roots were the tribes. The principles would form the constitution and the laws of the great Iroquois nation he would found. Hiawatha would preside over the first tribal council. The organization of the confederacy was mapped out on a long stick divided into five sections and fifty pegs, one for each member of the tribal council. A hundred years after his death, inspired revolutionary British colonists adopted many of Hiawatha's principles of good government in establishing a constitution of their own—the Constitution of the United States of America.

The Mystery of the Ohio Moundbuilders

Frederic Ward Putnam boarded a train in Boston. He was bound for Columbus, Ohio. The year was 1883. The Harvard archaeologist had read reports of strange geoglyphs—giant animal figures sculpted out of the earth and huge earthen mounds that rivaled Egypt's pyramids. He had to see them for himself.

As Putnam followed his guides through the thickets along the banks of Brush Creek, his heart beat fast in anticipation. He couldn't imagine that such colossal earthworks might exist in a wilderness like this, where there never was a city or any highly organized society.

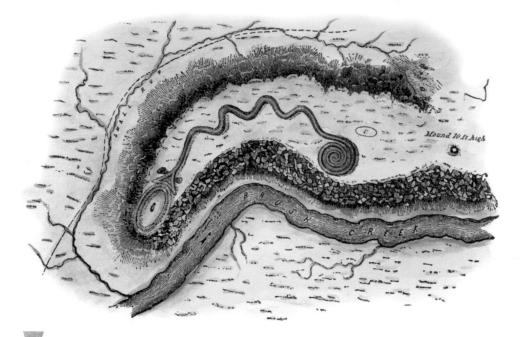

Ohio's famous Serpent Mound, near Cincinnati, is sculpted out of the bank of a creek.

As he reached the top of a cliff overlooking the river, he found himself climbing up a 5-foot-high zigzag hillside. He walked along the twisty 20-foot-wide slope, following its bends and turns for nearly a mile until it widened into the shape of a head. Then he realized that he was standing on a giant earth snake! Its head ended in what looked like a mouth open 75 feet wide. The snake appeared to have in its open jaws an oval shape half as long as a football field—a huge egg!

One hundred miles to the northeast, near the city of Newark, Putnam visited more earthworks. These looked more like figures out of a geometry book—gigantic enclosures in the shapes of circles and octagons, with gaps where the straight sides joined together. Some of the figures were connected together by narrow corridors, so people could walk from one space into another in a 4-square-mile area. The archaeologist encountered cone-shaped pyramids, also made out of earth. They must have been 75 feet high (as tall as a seven-story building) before they slowly began to erode over time. He saw Fort Ancient (near Cincinnati), a hilltop enclosure irregular in shape with gaps in the surrounding earth wall—just like those in the octagons.

Never had the professor seen such wondrous things—at least not in America. Here's what Professor Putnam wrote in his diary:

A HOPEWELL MEASURING STICK

Suppose you want to draw a geometrical shape. First you need to make some measurements. You get out a compass, a protractor, and a ruler. Because you want the figure to fit on a piece of 8-by-10-inch paper, you need to decide on a measuring unit—say, 4 inches. That will give the radius of a circle, or the side of a square, or the edge of an octagon. There is some pretty solid evidence the Hopewell did the same thing—except they weren't using paper. And their compass more likely was made out of a tall pole attached to long ropes.

Let's look at the evidence that suggests the Hopewell had a unit of measurement. The diameter of Newark's Observatory Circle is exactly 1,050 feet. The distance from the Observatory Mound on the edge of the circle to the center of the octagon is 2,100 feet. That's exactly 2 times 1,050 feet. Coincidence? Wait! The distance from the center of the Observatory Circle to the center of the Great Circle, located to the southeast, is exactly 6,300 feet, or 6 times 1,050 feet. That's also the distance from the Octagon to a square located in the same direction. This is not a coincidence. Old Caleb Atwater may have been correct: Whoever built the earthworks loved astronomy and geometry. And they seem to have brought them all together in their architecture, probably for religious purposes.

Some parts of the Newark Octagon/Circle Mound line up with the rising and setting positions of the sun and the moon at different times in their cycles.

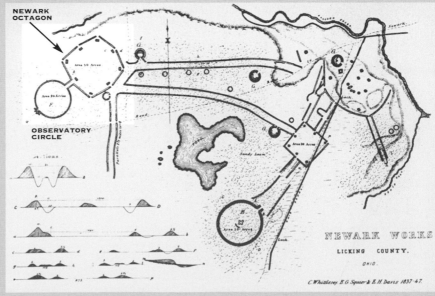

SERPENT MOUND

Radiocarbon dating (see page 114) tells us that the Hopewell people built the Serpent Mound sometime between 1025 and 1215 CE. There's no doubt that snakes were important to their culture. Archaeologists have excavated two snake effigies (a cultural likeness of a person or animal) made of stone inside Fort Ancient. As summer approaches, both align with the sunrise on the first day of summer. What do snakes have to do with the movement of the sun? Like the sun, snakes change with the seasons: They shed their skins. One early-eighteenth-century Ohio missionary wrote that the local natives believed a snake's gaze could hypnotize its prey. And because, like the sun, it comes out of the earth, a snake is considered the source of water and fertility. Too bad many people think all snakes are slimy creatures (they're not!) and associate them with evil things. Give a snake a break!

The most singular sensation of awe and admiration overwhelmed me . . . for here before me was the mysterious work of an unknown people. . . . I mused on the probabilities of the past; and there seemed to come to me a picture as of a distant time, of a people with strange customs, and with it came the demand for an interpretation of this mystery. The unknown must become known!

Today Ohio's famous earthworks may still be the most intriguing archaeological remains in North America. They are completely different from anything else we have found. And the ideas that have been proposed to explain why they were built are so distinct. They couldn't have been built by our Indians, thought Caleb Atwater, the postmaster of Circleville, Ohio, who was one of the first explorers of the ruins. He had written about them as early as 1820. The geometry is so perfect—perfect squares and circles and octagons. And the figures seem to line up with astronomical events that take place near the horizon. Whoever these people were—Caleb Atwater called them the Moundbuilders—they must have possessed a knowledge of math and astronomy that was much more advanced than the other tribes that lived in Ohio. Perhaps they were a lost civilization of prehistoric geniuses or vanished explorers! Or maybe the builders were a race of extinct giants? Who else would have had any use for such huge pyramids, big octagons, and a humongous snake?

True, these are all tantalizing suggestions, but to solve a cultural puzzle, you have to proceed like a detective who tries to solve a crime. First, you need hard evidence. Second, that evidence needs to be collected from many places. Third, and above all, convergence is the key—all the evidence needs to focus upon one solution to the problem. Atwater's old theories all have one thing in common: They lack the solid evidence that can come only from digging up and analyzing the artifacts.

Radiocarbon dating gives us a time element. (To find out how it works, turn to Chapter 9.) Changes in the style of artifacts point to changes in the culture that made them. But just how do we go about detecting changes in style? Suppose you collect cereal boxes. One day you open up a long-lost trunk in the attic and behold—a treasure trove of cereal boxes! Piled helter-skelter among them are some pretty old samples strewn among still older ones from the days of your grandparents, your great-grandparents, and so on. How would you go about finding ways to arrange them in order from the old-est to the most recent? One way might be by looking at the style of printing on the carton, or the presence of color, which would indicate a newer carton. Another way would be by identifying famous athletes who always seem to get themselves pictured on the boxes. Basically archaeologists do something similar with the artifacts they dig up—they look for clues that help to arrange the artifacts from oldest to newest based on style. When they do it with clay pots, they call it a ceramic sequence.

What do ceramic sequences have to do with the ancient earthworks? Take

EFFIGIES, EFFIGIES, EVERYWHERE!

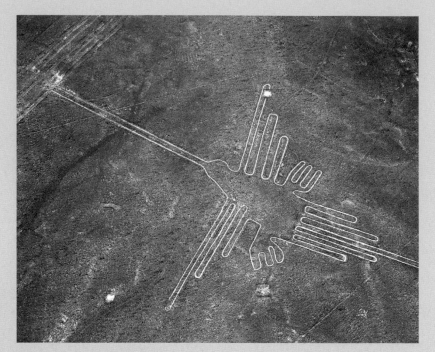

Like the banks of Ohio's rivers, the desert of Nasca, Peru, also has geoglyphs: a hummingbird (above) and an anhinga (right).

If you flew an airplane over the desert on the south coast of Peru, you would see a barren land. It looks like the surface of the moon until you come to the famous Nasca (**nass**-kuh) geoglyphs—huge drawings made on the earth, just as in Ohio. The desert, or pampa, as the local residents of the modern town of Nasca call it, is crisscrossed with a maze of lines—more than 700 of them.

There are also about 300 colossal trapezoids (triangles that have one point clipped off).

Nasca's pampa is also carved with zigzag scribbles, spirals, and about three dozen plant and animal figures. A long-necked bird is the largest of the pampa's carved creatures. It measures almost 2,000 feet from beak to tail feathers. It's probably an anhinga (ahn-**heen**-guh), the relative of a cormorant, a bird that lives on the coast where it hunts fish. The pampa artist who made the cormorant stretched its zigzag neck to imitate the wiggly motion the bird makes when it swallows a fish. Effigy figures like these are also found in Wisconsin (a long string of bear cubs) and in the desert near Blythe, California (the giant figure of a man). Many cultures of the world developed an interest in making giant earth drawings, or geoglyphs. We can't explain why, but we're fairly certain that the ones in Nasca have something to do with praying to the rain god. The geoglyphs seem to be focused upon places where water streams down from the high Andes Mountains into their parched environment. Remember that the Hopewell Serpent Mound also lies close to water.

the mounds, for instance. They turned out to be burial sites. When archaeologists made cuts or trenches through the Moundsville pyramid in eastern Ohio, they encountered ceramics decorated with different kinds of geometric designs in every layer they cut through. When radio-carbon-dated material was found in some of the layers, they could then connect *absolute* dates to different parts of the *relative* dates on the ceramic sequence. To go back to the cereal boxes, we may know that Babe Ruth came before Wayne Gretzky, who came before Serena Williams—that's relative dating. But if we know the birth date of one of them, that helps us to arrive at an absolute ("true") chronology.

Copper effigy of a bird. Can you identify it?

The burial mounds are like hotels of the dead. (Archaeologists call them charnel houses.) The Moundbuilders stored their ancestors in boxes or on mats in roofed compartments next to one another, with doorways at opposite ends. More elaborate accommodations were reserved for wealthier people. One burial uncovered by archaeologists contained four adults and two infants covered with pearls and surrounded by hundreds of copper, mica, silver, and tortoiseshell ornaments. These must have been people of high status, perhaps a local chief and his family.

The archaeologists also encountered little animal figures

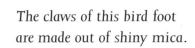

The claws of this bird foot are made out of shiny mica.

This Hopewell effigy pipe is shaped like an animal that was as familiar to them as it is to us.

(including a snake) made out of mica, spoons made out of tortoiseshell, and baskets of dried corn for survival in the world of the dead. Some of the skulls of the dead were deformed. They probably tied boards to children's foreheads to mold their skulls into a long shape, for the same reason we pierce our ears—to look cool!

As archaeologists dug deeper into the layers cut by their trenches—and therefore deeper into the past of the Moundbuilders—they began to detect changes in the shapes of the flint points. They also noted changes in the way the dead were positioned and decorated. For example, physical anthropologists found peck marks made by birds' beaks on some of the earliest skeletons. This could mean that the bodies were left out so that vultures and hawks could strip away the flesh before the final burial. Later in history (higher up in the trench), the Moundbuilders seem to have given up this practice.

The archaeological record tells us that Ohio's earliest Moundbuilders were a people called the Adena (uh-**dee**-nuh). They occupied the Ohio River Valley from 500 BCE to 200 CE. Their ancestors had actually begun to build mounds and enclosures in Louisiana as early as 3400 BCE at sites like Watson Brake and 1500 BCE in Poverty Point. When the Adena migrated to the north and mixed with natives there, they brought that idea with them. The Hopewell (100 BCE–500 CE) were the major architects of Ohio's mounds.

A GIANT CALENDAR WITHOUT WRITING

Suppose you couldn't write or count. How would you keep track of time? One way might be to line up sticks to mark the changing place of sunrise or sunset on the horizon during the course of the year. One stick might mark where the sun comes up on New Year's Day, another on Valentine's Day, and another on your birthday. Or you could organize your house (or temple) to align with the sun on key dates of the year, like when the rainy season is due or when the sun god begins to return from his winter home in the south.

Archaeoastronomers study the arrangement and orientation of things people build. When they studied the Ohio mounds, they found that some of the circle and octagon sites are aligned with the sun's yearly cycle by marking where the sun rises and sets on the first days of summer and winter. Some also align with the moon, which takes nineteen years to complete its orbit. For example, there's a mound on the southwestern end of the Newark Octagon/Circle. If you stand on it, you can look directly along the axis from the circle through the narrow connector to the octagon. There you will still see the full moon rise at its southernmost extreme. This may have been a sign that it was time for the people to assemble inside the sacred spaces of the octagon/circle to worship the moon god.

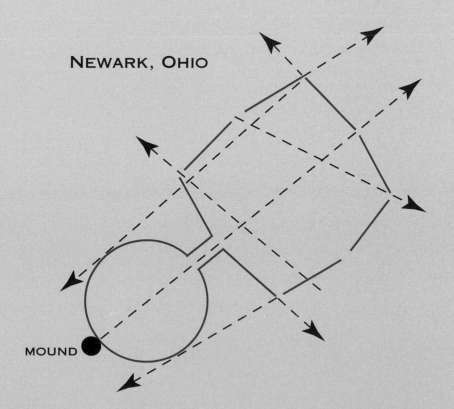

NEWARK, OHIO

MOUND

Some lines, shown here by arrows, between key points on the Hopewell octagon/circle in Newark, Ohio, point to where the moon rises and sets at different times in its cycle. Try measuring the relationship between the circle and the octagon discussed on page 49.

Watching the sun set over spaces between mounds was a way of marking out the seasons.

They constructed hundreds of geometrical earthworks along the northern tributaries of the Ohio River. Ohio archaeologists who have excavated the early Hopewell village of High Bank think a few extended families—say, one hundred people at most—lived in the dozen or so huts that once made up this settlement. People cleared a patch of land and planted small cornfields. After five years or so—once they used up all the local firewood, exhausted the soil, and filled up the garbage dump—they pulled up stakes and moved on.

Now here's the greatest Hopewell mystery of all: Where did small groups of villages get all the human energy required to construct such elaborate structures? We don't yet know the answer. Archaeologists have no evidence that Hopewell people had slaves or armies, or even kings and nobles.

But cultures we *do* know something about can offer some clues about the building timescale. For example, history teaches us that medieval people took generations to build the huge cathedrals of Europe. It may seem weird to us, but, for them, the *process* of building a cathedral was as important as the *product*—the cathedral itself. The same was likely true of Egypt's pyramids. In both cases, the reason behind the project was religion—a powerful force. So maybe the energy required to build the mounds was spread over a long period of time. Still, despite Professor Putnam's resolve, the exact reasons why the Hopewell chose the forms of circles and octagons and why they aligned them so precisely with the heavens may forever remain unknown.

Finally, let's not think of Adena, Hopewell, and Mississippian people as different and distinct from one another. Instead, we should imagine them as blends of people who changed culture through time. Just look at how our immigrant population has changed. Early-nineteenth-century North Americans were mostly English-Scotch-Irish. If you could go back in a time machine and talk to one of them, you probably wouldn't be able to tell whether the person lived in the British Isles or Virginia. (See Chapter 9 to find out how linguists study language changes.) And it's a good bet you'd have a hard time understanding much of the conversation because of the person's accent. On the other hand, a century later, early-twentieth-century Americans had lots of Scandinavian, German, and Italian characteristics. Still later, immigrants to the New World were of Latin American descent. As these people mixed and intermarried, the customs of their cultures got mixed, too. They changed the way they dressed and talked—and even the way they prepared their food. Today's North America is more diverse than ever. It is 3 percent Asian, 11 percent Latin American, and 12 percent African American. Fewer than 1 percent claim Native American descent. Being American today is very different from what it meant when the Pilgrims came over on the *Mayflower*!

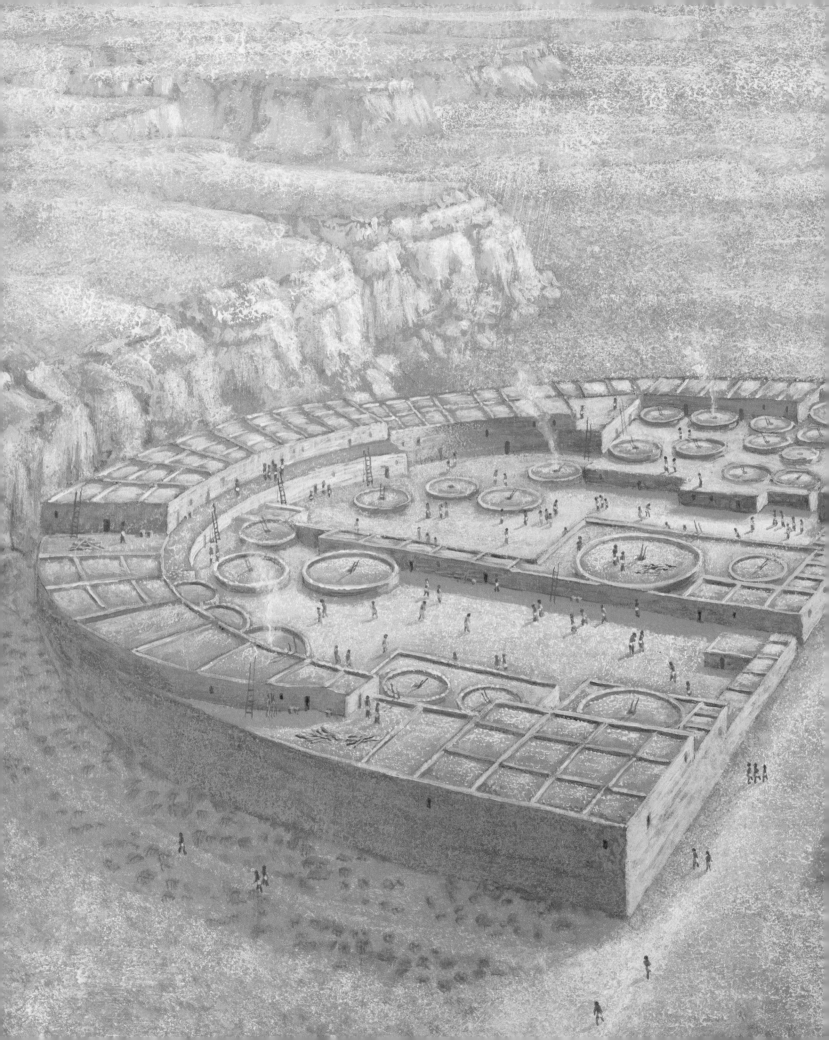

The Anasazi

Why is a 3-acre-large building hidden between the walls of desolate Chaco Canyon near the southwest Four Corners area, where the states of Arizona, New Mexico, Utah, and Colorado meet? It's shaped like a huge capital D. The outside of the D is covered by a checkerboard roof situated over a 660-room apartment complex. Inside the D are thirty-two circles of different sizes, each pierced by a hole. If you weren't seeing this picture in a book about Native Americans, you might guess Pueblo Bonito ("Beautiful Town," as the Spanish named it) would be a great hiding place for a colony of alien astronauts.

Reconstruction of an ancient Anasazi kiva (top). This wall painting in a kiva (bottom) tells you something about the religious rituals practiced there.

Pueblo Bonito is actually a planned village—one of about a hundred villages built in the eleventh century by the Anasazi (ah-nuh-**sah**-zee), the ancestors of today's Pueblo Indians, and distant descendants of the ancient Beringian migrations.

Until the nineteenth century, Pueblo Bonito was the biggest apartment house in the Americas! More than 1,000 people once lived there. Then, in the fourteenth century, it was suddenly abandoned, probably because of overpopulation. Tree ring studies tell us a drought may have been involved as well.

Climb down the ladder into one of the round, pitlike structures—it's called a kiva (**kee**-vuh)—and you'll be convinced that it has a lot more to do with religion than fantasy space travel. Archaeologists have excavated a kiva wall painting at the Kuaua (koo-**ah**-wuh), New Mexico, pueblo. It shows the god of lightning using his spear to pierce the sky to make rain fall. Lightning bolts and seeds come out of his mouth. An eagle soars next to him. The wall of the kiva had been plastered and painted over

GROWING UP NAVAJO

Some Arab cultures have a coming-of-age face-painting ritual. Young women mark a line with black eyeliner from the center of their lower lip down to the bottom of their chin. They center the line on four dots. This marks their entrance into womanhood. Bat mitzvah and confirmation are two more familiar religious celebrations today that also signal an important stage in a girl's growing up. Anthropologists call them puberty rites. Studying religious rites among present-day descendants of the ancient people of the Southwest can give us some clues about how the Anasazi once behaved. This is because the Navajo, Hopi, and Apache, who mixed with the Anasazi and then replaced them, are known for hanging on to tradition.

Every year in northern Arizona, Navajo boys and girls aged seven to thirteen are initiated into the Night Way chant. The initiation part of the ceremony begins when the kids are led out of the tepee into the light of the campfire. Next, two figures with scary masks—Grandfather of the Monsters and Grandmother of Creation—come before them. As the children tremble, Grandmother sings a chant in a high-pitched voice as she places cornmeal on the girls' shoulders. Grandfather strikes the boys with a bundle of reeds. Then they take off their masks and put them over the faces of the children. This shows the children that they are impersonators and not real monsters. Like our Santa Claus ritual, it's a secret older children must keep from younger ones who haven't yet been initiated.

You might think you'd be fortunate to be a young Navajo person. Today some Navajo moms and dads are very permissive. They may let their kids stay up late, eat what they want—even throw temper tantrums. Toilet training isn't important. "The baby knows what is best" is one of their sayings. But in other ways you'd need to be very responsible. For example, by the age of six you'd be expected to water the animals, gather twigs for the fire, and help tend the sheep. If you're a preteen girl you'd need to participate in Kinaalda, the Changing Woman Ceremony. First you are put on a special four-day diet. Then you must do an all-night "sing." Last comes the Molding Ceremony. Your mom kneads your body like a ball of dough to make you beautiful and shapely— just like Changing Woman, the women's favorite of all the Anasazi holy people.

Mesa Verde, Colorado. This cliff dwelling offered both safety and shelter to its inhabitants.

dozens of times. We can be sure that the kivas were used for religious ceremonies—in this case, one that involved rainmaking—because the living descendants of the Anasazi still use them, though they wish to keep what goes on inside secret from outsiders.

The Anasazi could anticipate when to prepare for their seasonal festivals, such as the rainmaking ceremony, because they had an official sun-watching priest who memorized the places where the sun rose at different times of the year. He watched the rugged vertical mountain peaks that could be seen in the distance. As recently as the nineteenth century, the Zuni pekwin sat at his sun-watching station at the top of the mesa. The main corn-planting ceremony

WERE THE ANASAZI CANNIBALS?

"See these thin parallel grooves running across the jawline?" said archaeologist Christy Turner. "They were made by a flint knife." The skull was one of dozens of bone fragments excavated at the Chaco apartment complex. The skull belonged to a child between six and eight years old, and it had been violently smashed. "And these vertebrae . . . they were pulverized with a large stone to get at the marrow inside. The clincher," adds Turner, "is that the process is exactly the same as the one the Anasazi used to butcher and cook antelope and prairie dog, two of their staple foods." The archaeologists also found coprolites, remains of human feces, at the same site. They detected no plant remains in these samples, which suggests the meal eaten by that person consisted solely of meat. Strangely enough, they didn't find hair or ground bone material in the samples—proof again that only the flesh was consumed.

Could starvation have driven the Anasazi to eat one another? Or could it have been warfare and political terrorism? Some warfare rituals demanded that the enemy be eaten as a sign of intimidation—to demonstrate to the living relatives of the victims that they have been conquered. But other archaeologists believe the violent treatment of the bones might have had nothing to do with eating the remains. It could all be part of a dismemberment ritual. Many southwestern tribes used to dismember people who were found guilty of practicing witchcraft. More digging at Chaco may help answer this difficult question.

Archaeologist Christy Turner examines Anasazi bones to determine what happened at Chaco Canyon.

CERAMICS AND CULTURE: THE MIMBRES POTTERS

Ceramics are one way of distinguishing one culture from another. The Mogollon (**muh**-guh-yon), an Anasazi-influenced people who lived along the Mimbres (**mim**-bruhs) River of southern New Mexico between 1000 and 1150 CE, made some of the most beautiful American ceramics. The pieces were distinct—black on white painted clay with thin-line geometric decorations around the outside and an animal painted on the inside. It could be a fish, a bird, a bird eating a fish, an armadillo, or even an unusual-looking bug. No two pieces are alike. The Mogollon "killed" their pots by punching a hole through the bottoms when they buried them with their dead.

took place four days after the summer solstice, when the rising sun reached its farthest point to the north along the eastern horizon.

Archaeologists have found other artifacts in kivas. There's always a central fire pit and usually a couple of sweatboxes. In the sweatbox, worshippers would pour water over heated rocks. Climbing inside the chamber, they would use the steam to purify their bodies. They believed that this made it easier to come into contact with sacred spirits.

The early Anasazi were nomads. Anthropologists call them the Basketmakers because, by 300 CE, they had mastered that craft. By 500 CE, they were making pottery. Once they learned to plant beans, corn, and squash, they realized the advantages of settling in small villages. Their first houses were simple pits covered with mud plaster. The mud helped save energy by absorbing sunlight and keeping in the heat.

The longer you stay in one place,

the more home improvements you tend to make. The Anasazi began to dig their pits deeper, and they faced them with sandstone walls quarried out of the 800-foot-high cliffs of the canyon. They added on other rooms and joined their houses to those of their neighbors. Building narrow hallways at the entrances to the houses created better air circulation. Also, the draft drove smoke out of the hole in the roof. Next to the fire pit, they dug a hole so that their dead ancestors could enter their residences. They built well-insulated circular storage pits behind their houses to keep the harvested crops safe for the winter. Once Anasazi men discovered that these structures stayed cool in the summer and warm in the winter, they developed the round underground pit into the kiva. By 900 CE, Anasazi houses had become rather elaborate places.

The village of Pueblo Bonito grew out of several of these pit houses linked together in a curved pattern. Think of it as a huge longhouse with a bend in it. The inside part of the curve faces south. That cut off the fierce north wind. It also gave maximum exposure to the low sun in winter. As the population grew, the curve got longer. Second stories were added. By 1300 CE, the population increased to several hundred. As a result, the Anasazi needed to cultivate and irrigate more land by digging ditches to divert water that ran down the canyon walls in the rainy season. Eventually the entire canyon floor was covered with thousands of gardens. By learning to irrigate, the townspeople were able to feed more people, but that then attracted even more people to the town. Like the centers of many of our cities, Pueblo Bonito began to go downhill; there were too many people living in too little space. Then nature played a cruel trick on the Anasazi.

Climate and collapse—it's a topic of debate among archaeologists today. We've all seen the damage hurricanes can do to the U.S. coastal areas and the

Caribbean islands. We all know about the powerful volcanic explosion of Mount St. Helens. Many people of the West Coast live in fear of big earthquakes. And who hasn't heard about the threat of global warming? Paleoclimatologists have devised many ways to learn about what the climate was like in the past. You can learn about many of them in Chapter 9. They study the growth of tree rings—the bigger the ring, the wetter the climate for that year. They examine the percentage of radioactive oxygen to normal oxygen in sediments cored from ancient lake bottoms. It works just like the radiocarbon dating method. Precipitation (rainfall) adds water, and evaporation takes it away. Paleoclimatologists measure the ratio of evaporation to precipitation in a core sample. This ratio is high when there's a lot of rain and low when there are drought conditions. They also collect and classify different kinds of pollens in the cores they collect. This helps them to determine what kinds of plants the pollen came from—and whether these plants grow best in a wet or dry environment. Finally, they study soil erosion. Though soil wears away gradually, erosion happens much faster when rainfall is excessive.

The scientific evidence from all of these studies leaves no doubt that our southwestern states experienced a 200-year-long dry period that helped wipe out an already troubled Anasazi culture. It was all a case of bad timing. The droughts began about 1150 CE. As they persisted, the people became restless. "Why haven't our priests succeeded in persuading the lightning-maker god to intervene?" they may have asked. "Perhaps we haven't been making the proper offerings?" Families and clans quarreled. "What has happened to our prosperous life?" "Why is my crop drying up?" "How will I feed my children?" "We need stronger leaders!" Some Anasazi revolted, while others began to leave the area. The Navajo, the next wave of nomadic wanderers,

moved in. Bloods blended. Languages and customs mixed. Just as in modern cities, the ethnic makeup of the Chaco Canyon population changed. The "Chaco Phenomenon" had come to an end.

Today there are lots of Chaco mysteries left to solve. Where did they bury their dead? No cemeteries have been found. Why did they build long, straight roads that seem to lead to nowhere? And why weren't the Anasazi more influenced by the Toltec (**tohl**-tek) and the Totonac (**toe**-toe-nak)—neighboring peoples of Mexico who built large cities? While we can admire the Anasazi for their successful experiment in apartment living, we are left to wonder about the greatest Chaco mystery of all: Why would people choose to live in what looks to us like a hostile place? But then, those of us who tempt nature by living in earthquake and hurricane zones do exactly the same. Perhaps we should ask ourselves the same question.

A model of an Anasazi village. What reasons would people have to make a cliff dwelling like this one in Mesa Verde, Colorado (500–700 BCE)?

Natives of the Northwest Coast

 What gifts did you get for your last birthday? Which had the most value? Who gave them to you? When was the last time you gave someone a really big gift? What gift did you give? Was it a precious possession of yours that you gave up? Was it something you made with your own hands? And—be honest—do you *really* enjoy giving gifts as much as receiving them?

Most of us would offer similar answers to each of these questions. The most costly gifts we receive usually come from those closest to us—our parents, maybe a favorite aunt or uncle—especially those who can afford to purchase expensive presents.

This ceremonial robe worn by a person of high status would have made an ideal potlatch present.

The Kwakiutl (kwah-kee-**ooh**-tuhl) Indians are among the descendants of the people of the great migrations who live on the Northwest Coast. They took gift-giving—or, as they called it, pot-latching—to a very high level:

"Haha Hahane!" Now he gave away four other blankets, ten marten blankets, seven black bear blankets, thirty-five mink blankets, and fifty deerskin blankets. . . . As soon as he had finished his potlatch, he told the [guests] that he had changed his name. You will call me Lalelit. . . . I am full of names and privileges. . . . I have many chiefs as ancestors all over the world; and I feel like laughing at what is said by the lower chiefs, when they claim to belong to the chief, my ancestor.

WHAT ARE TOTEM POLES?

Totem poles are famous among the Indians of the Northwest Coast. A totem is basically a symbol that tells about the mystical relationship between animals and a group of people. Totem poles are not objects of worship, as early missionaries who destroyed many of them once believed. They might better be called "memorial poles." Northwesterners were skilled wood-carvers, and this is how they represented their clan history and family background, or lineage. They believed their descent went back to the animals that still serve as their guides or advisors. For example, Raven Clan members might carve a raven on top of a totem. Most totem poles were proudly displayed on the beach in front of the village. Some were door or wall posts in houses, and some poles were designed to hold the ashes of the deceased.

Many of the animal designs carved on totem poles were also woven into blankets by the women. The weaver would begin her task by spinning goat's wool and fibers from the bark of cedar trees into yarn. Then she'd dye the yarn blue-green (a favorite color), yellow, and black. Finally, she would weave the designs. As on the totem poles, all figures should be viewed from the front. (Viewing anything from the side would be offensive!) That's why the animal figures in their art always look flattened and symmetrical. These beautiful blankets were highly prized at potlatches. Anyone who could afford to pay a weaver for the six months it took to make a blanket would certainly be regarded as a high-status individual!

What creatures can you identify in the family history on this clan's totem pole?

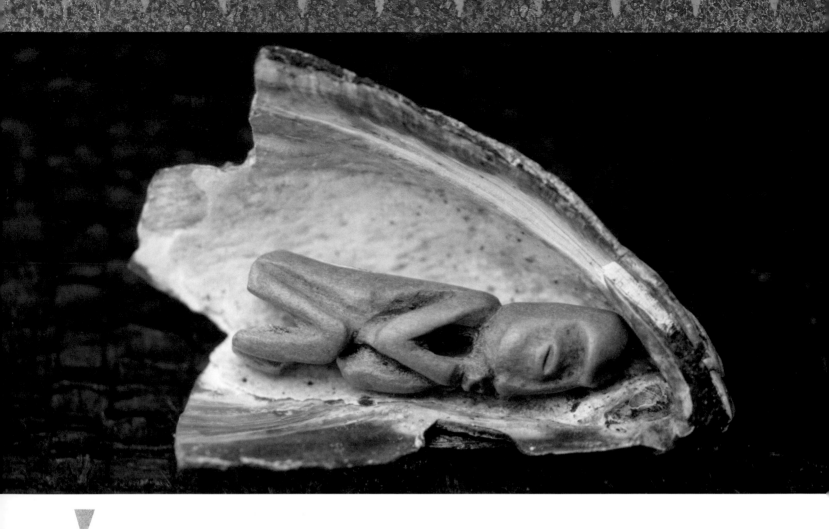

This carved figure of a child is inlaid into a mussel shell that is shaped like a spear point.

Those words were spoken more than one hundred years ago by one of the wealthiest members of the Whale Clan. He was throwing a party that he'd been planning for more than a year! He had already dispatched special messengers to invite the 200 guests. They must have time to hollow out, paint, and decorate their canoes so they'd look good when they arrived by sea at the potlatch. He asked members of the Raven Clan to attend as special guests. They must prepare themselves by practicing a special song and dance that told about their lineage. They would compete with the Whale Clan to see who performed the best.

Meanwhile, the hosts would decorate the Great House with fresh wall paintings of the ancestor gods, woven baskets, and blankets. They would make new hats and robes to wear and a new staff for the local Whale Clan leader. The party would last twelve days. There would be lots to eat—salmon and venison, stews and seaweed, berries and fish oil—all of it served in huge dishes and eaten with giant spoons. They would drink from huge, decorated cups.

Toward the end of the feast, the host would shower gifts on all who attended. Low-ranking guests received blankets made out of cedar bark. High-ranking guests received canoes and mink blankets. The gifts represented many seasons of hard work. As the wealthy chief gave out the gifts, he would recite the history of each one—where it came from, who made it, and how old it was. He would take special care to tell about the value of each of his gifts.

Potlatch is all about validating status, which is the term anthropologists use for proving your high rank. You do it not only by showing off your wealth but also by giving much of it away. As a culture that appreciates material wealth, we realize that the Kwakiutl, the Tlingit (tuh-**leen**-giht), the Haida (**hay**-duh), and other northwest natives from Alaska to Oregon who potlatched aren't so different from anyone who throws a big birthday party or an elaborate open house today. When the chiefs of the Raven Clan and their rival Whale Clan accepted the local chief's gifts—when they became the new owners of the holdings of the chief's ancient lineage—they weren't just bonding with the chief's family. They were showing respect by giving him the right to the rank he claimed—his descent from ancestor chiefs all around the world—and to his new name.

The guests knew what they were getting into, for there was a second purpose to the potlatch. It had to do with gift-giving, and it is practiced all over the world—even in our culture.

Every gift demands reciprocity, which means giving a gift in return.

HUNTING THE KILLER WHALE

Scana (**skah**-nuh), the Haida call it—the spirit that lives inside of a killer whale and makes him so fierce. They tell the legend of the young boys who first caught sight of the killer whale. For fun, they threw stones at him. One of the stones damaged the whale's dorsal fin. As he headed for the beach, the boys tried to flee. He changed himself into a man in a canoe and scolded the boys: "How'd you like it if I damaged your canoe?" He showed them his dorsal fin, magically transformed into the broken side of his canoe. He shamed the boys into repairing it. Then he changed back into his whale shape and returned to the sea. Since then, the Indians have shown great respect for all whales. They have learned to value every part of its body—the meat that they eat (the skin is a delicacy), the tough muscles that give them their rope, the intestines they use to make containers, and the blubber and oil that serve them as both food and fuel to burn in their lamps.

Gray whale hunting is a very dangerous activity. The canoe in which the whaler and six or eight of his companions set sail is dwarfed by the beast they are hunting. They must paddle fast because, once alongside, the chief harpooner gets only one shot! He fires his 18-foot-long spear. It is tipped with a razor-sharp mussel shell backed up by a barbed bone spur to keep the spear secure once it gets lodged in its target. When the harpoon is implanted, the whaler throws the floats over the side. The floats are made of inflated sealskin and attached to the harpoon by a rope made out of dried muscle. That slows down the whale as he tries to escape so that harpooners in the other boats can launch a side attack. It also keeps the whale afloat once he dies.

Hunting whales takes special skills and lots of cooperation.

Reciprocity happens at parties when we exchange gifts with friends and loved ones. Among the Kwakiutl, the next potlatch given by a clan member will ensure that all the goods will be properly redistributed. Distributing wealth by rank is part of the tradition in this culture. It will offer someone else an opportunity to claim his/her status in public—and that's good for bonding people together.

The Kwakiutl could potlatch for lots of reasons. For example, you could have a gift party to mourn the passing of a chief or to bond the relatives of bride and groom together. It could be an occasion for a totem-raising ceremony—or you could challenge someone who insulted you to a gift-for-gift matching contest, in which rivals took turns trashing their personal property in public, piece by piece! The loser would be the first one to run out of stuff to destroy.

Extravagant potlatching like this could happen only in a very wealthy culture. The Northwest Coast Indians lived not only at the edge of an ocean abundant with life—like shellfish, salmon, and whales—but also on land that offered elk, mountain goats, and berries. And because they were outstanding long-distance traders, they could get their hands on exotic goods like copper and jade from the mountains that hugged the coast.

The more you have, the more you want. That may be why some wealthy

Before entering this Haida longhouse on Queen Charlotte Island, British Columbia, you pass through a doorway decorated with images of the ancestors.

TREASURE IN A MUDSLIDE

It was a hot summer night in the fifteenth-century seaside village of Ozette (on Washington State's coast). The Makah had lived there for decades. Their name means "generous with food." Nestled up against the steep hills, they had access to fish that moved in fast-flowing streams and to plants and animals that thrived just a short climb up the mountain. Rain had been falling for days, but now it had finally stopped, and a bright, full moon glistened on the rippling water. The embers from the fire under the now-empty salmon-smoking rack glowed faintly. Most of the young children had gone to

sleep. An elder craftsperson was putting the finishing touches on an item for next month's potlatch to which the Makah had been invited. He was inlaying prized sea otter teeth into a carved wooden whale fin. This gift would proclaim his mastery over the greatest of all wealth of the sea. His son was fastening a sharp harpoon head onto the shaft of a long lance used to spear whales.

Meanwhile, his eldest daughter gently rubbed whale oil on the surface of a spooky face mask to make it shiny so her dad would stand out when he danced at the party. The girl's aunt had just finished working on the loom and was putting away her weaving tools for the night in her corner of the house.

Suddenly the quiet of the night was jarred by a low, rumbling sound. Thousands of tons of mud cascaded down the hillside. The young girl dropped the mask and flew out the door, only to find herself caught in an ooze of mud as high as her waist. She was among the lucky few to escape the blanket of mud that would seal the entire village that night, turning it into an airless tomb.

The Makah tragedy turned out to be a treasure for archaeologists who later came to explore Ozette after a local person reported seeing a strange-looking canoe paddle sticking out of the sand. The Ozette legacy has yielded 65,000 artifacts in perfect condition—they had been sealed in mud for 500 years!

people develop a desire for more and more material things. Native Americans of the Northwest were constantly feuding over property. They would send raiding parties off to another's turf, and the winners would proudly display the belongings they brought back. This might include slaves from a defeated village. They let the slaves live in the master's house. Slaves were even allowed to marry and have kids, but their children would become slaves, too. Sometimes the slaves were sacrificed and buried under a totem pole or house post to show that prestigious people could afford to dispense with such valuable property.

The archaeological record tells us that the people of the Northwest Coast had access to this environmental wealth ever since they migrated there from farther north between 8000 BCE and 3000 BCE, when the glacial ice had almost totally melted. Archaeologists have found tons of surplus goods and exotic items stowed away in graves: mountain goat–hair blankets, copper-and-shell decorations, and masks elaborately carved out of different kinds of wood. They were probably potlatching as early as 500 CE.

A Day in the Strange Life of the Timucua

They wrestled alligators, hunted with blow-guns, and tattooed their bodies from head to toe. They were the fierce Timucua (tih-muh-coo-uh) of central and northern Florida. One of several related tribes whose ancestors migrated across the Bering land bridge, these Native Americans lived on the southeast coastal plain between Louisiana and North Carolina in the sixteenth century. Let's visit one of their villages and discover why they seemed so mysterious to the French explorer Jacques LeMoyne, the first outsider to encounter them.

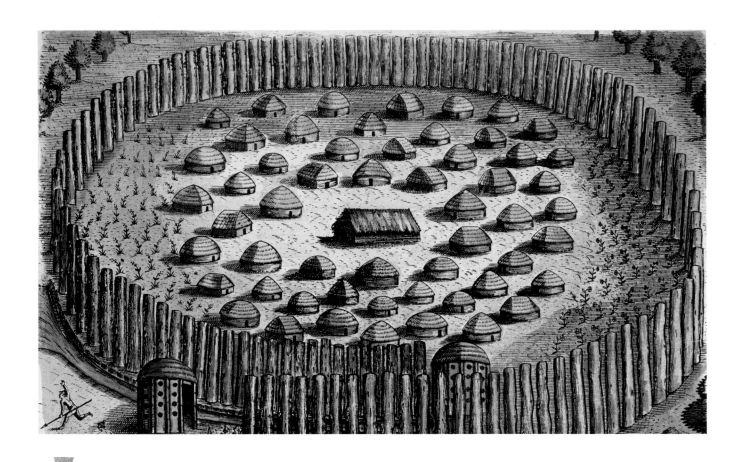

The commoners' huts
surrounded the chief's house
in this stockade model of a
late-sixteenth-century
Timucua village in Florida.

In 1564, LeMoyne wrote a beautifully illustrated book that
has given us the only impressions of a people who have now
completely disappeared. They were as unusual to him as aliens
from another planet might be to us.

It's a steamy afternoon when we enter the gate of the circular Timucua village. As we pass between the two guardhouses and then
around the wooden palisades that encircle the settlement, we catch our first
glimpse of the round huts the Timucua live in. There are about fifty of them
inside the fence, each large enough to accommodate a family of six or eight.
The large, rectangular building at the center is where council meetings are held.

This warrior wears a special headdress, a metal pendant called a gorget around his neck, and cymbals around his knees and elbows that jangle when he walks. The woman wears a grass skirt draped from her shoulder to her knees. But what's really unique about both this particular man and woman is that they are covered with tattoos. The tattoos are a code that tells a person's status in the tribe. Tattooing is a very painful process. A tattoo expert pricks the skin with sharp needles. He dips them in poisonous mercuric oxide, also called cinnabar, for red, and finely powdered charcoal for black—the Timucua's favorite colors. Anyone found with tattoos that lied about their status was forced to remove them—which wasn't easy!

On the other side of the village, we can see some men preparing a barbecue. They smoke meat by laying it on wooden racks supported by forked posts high above a smoldering fire. Slowly drying out the meat keeps it from spoiling. Dried out, tasty

A Timucua man and woman. He is heavily tattooed and wears many body ornaments, signs of his high status. She wears a long metal necklace and carries a bowl of maize.

strips of barbecued alligator meat will last for weeks. What's on the rack? Unusual-looking shapes for cuts of meat. Look closely! You can see some whole fish, pieces of turkey, hunks of bear meat, a few lizards, parts of a wildcat, and, yes, an entire alligator!

This drawing made in the fifteenth century by one of the first outsiders to visit a Timucua village shows natives tending to a barbecue. Can you tell what's cooking?

The chief emerges from his large hut for an afternoon stroll. He wears a fancy hat and a long deerhide robe. His neck and knees are decorated with beaded bracelets. An attendant carries the end of his robe so it won't get soiled. Two slaves fan the king of the Timucua to keep him cool. His three wives follow along behind. He is an important Timucua chief. His name is Saturiwa (sah-tuh-**ree**-wuh), and he rules over thirty neighboring villages as well as his own. Tomorrow Saturiwa will lead a council of war against his hostile neighbors to the north. A runner who arrived here last night told him of the attack on one of his outlying villages. He says he witnessed the enemy taking arms, legs, and scalps of the defeated people back to their home meeting ground. The runner followed them, and peeking through the palisades, he saw them hoist the body parts on poles in a victory celebration. Then their dancing shaman cursed Saturiwa.

The king will be up well before dawn tomorrow. He will put on his shell-and-copper sun medallions. He will take his bow and gather his archers at the center of the village. The war ritual will begin with a drinking ceremony to strengthen their bodies for the task that lies ahead of them. The women will brew a strong herb tea—so strong it makes you sweat. Warriors who can't keep it down will not be allowed to join the war party. Then Saturiwa will fill a large wooden plate with water. The great chief will turn toward the sun to bless the water. Then he will throw the water into the air and utter these words to his army—words that he has spoken many times before: "As I have done with the water, so I pray that you may do with the blood of your enemies."

Saturiwa and his wife go for a walk. Their attendants carry fans on poles. She has several ladies-in-waiting.

The archers are Saturiwa's special forces. They are expert marksmen. They will tie flaming Spanish moss to their arrows and fire them at the huts of the enemy villagers. Their assistants will carry clubs for fighting in close quarters.

Inspired by the water ritual, Saturiwa's archers surround an enemy village.

They will sharpen their fingernails into points to gouge out the enemy's foreheads so the blood will flow into their eyes and blind them. Yes, tomorrow will be an eventful day in the land of the Timucua!

If you were a Timucua alligator hunter, all you'd need is a 10-foot pole, a few clubs, a few friends, and a lot of patience. You perch with five or six fellow alligator hunters in a thatched hut by the riverside, waiting for a hungry alligator to come to the shoreline. The beast crawls along in shallow water at the edge of the bank with its mouth open in search of food. Once you spot it, each of your cohorts holds a section of the pole. The creature comes closer—still closer. Timing is important. When the alligator turns and faces you, you all run at full speed toward it and jam the pole as far as you can down its throat. The creature writhes and flips. You twist the pole and try to overturn it. Once you flip it over on its back, the rest of the group descend on the beast and club it to death. When you're sure the alligator is dead, you hoist it up on your backs and carry it to the barbecue.

The Timucua barbecue came from a southeastern Native American invention that goes back at least 4,000 years—the pit barbecue. Archaeologists excavating at Poverty Point, Louisiana, have found underground ovens, about the size of an oven in a modern stove, filled with ash and char, along with clay objects of different shapes. These "cooking balls" were heated in a fire and then placed in the pit over a layer of fish, meat, and vegetables wrapped in wet palmetto leaves. These lay on top of a bed of hot coals. Then the whole feast, like a modern clambake, was covered with more wet leaves for insulation and buried. Total cooking time: about twelve hours.

Hunting wild animals required clever strategies. Here we see alligator hunters in action.

Today, five centuries after the great Saturiwa fought his war, few artifacts remain. But, when archaeologist David Hurst Thomas broke through the floor of the remains of an old mission church on an island off the coast of Georgia in 1982, he was amazed to find 432 graves of seventeenth-century descendants of the Timucua. They had been uprooted from their native tribes, captured as slaves, and relocated by colonists. Their bones tell the story of the difficult lives they led, laboring under their captors. The holes in the eye sockets of some skulls come from iron-deficiency anemia. It probably resulted from a diet of mostly corn and too little protein, plus bad sanitation. Bent arm and thigh bones and wear and

HOW RELIGION MIXED WITH MEDICINE

The Timucua didn't believe in one humanlike god who created them in his own image. They had many gods, and though the gods possessed supernatural powers, they lived, like people, in the natural world. The world of the Creek, who lived in Georgia, was filled with supernatural creatures. Birds, bears, deer, and all kinds of snakes—horned snakes, sky snakes, water snakes—all had special powers of their own.

The "knowers," or prophets, taught the people about religion. They knew all about the weather and the diagnosis of disease. Once a knower made the diagnosis, he turned the person over to a "fasting man," who knew the specific cure that was matched with each cause. These healers fasted in order to have visions, which told them how to make people well.

Most cures would start with a sweatbath. Then the patient would be laid out with his/her head to the east, surrounded by insignias of red, green, black, and white, one in each of the four directions. The fasting man would make a brew out of the proper herbs. He would blow it through a little blowgun onto the patient's body. He would rub it into the skin. Then the patient would drink some of the infusion. For particularly difficult cases, the curer might need to make small cuts in the sick person's body, then use his blowgun to suck out the evil spirits. Like our great heart and brain surgeons, successful fasting men were greatly admired. But, like anyone who had knowledge of supernatural powers, they were also feared and sometimes even regarded with suspicion. In some instances when a curer failed, he might be beaten to death by angry relatives!

Sweathouses were used to purify and to drive out disease. They work like a sauna. You enter a sealed tent, or hut, containing heated rocks. After working up a sweat, you dive into a nearby cold creek. This photograph of a Siwash sweathouse was taken in Oregon.

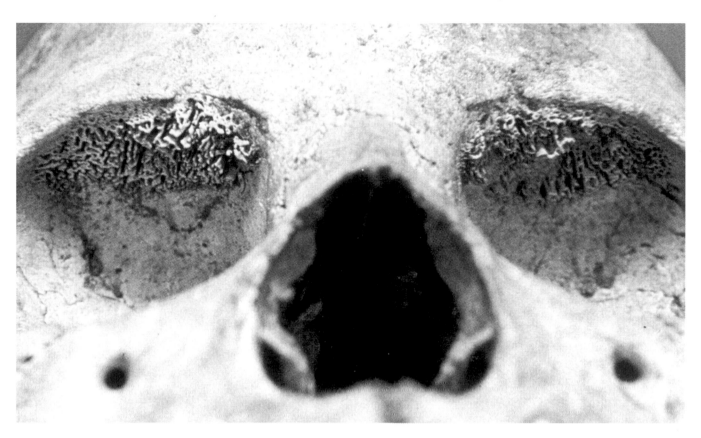

tear on the vertebrae of the spines of other skeletons prove they spent their lives carrying heavy loads. We know these Indians worked on building projects and toiled in the fields for long hours. As one colonist wrote at the time: "All of the natives . . . suffer . . . injuries from the fact that the governors, lieutenants, and soldiers oblige them to carry loads on their shoulders."

Check out the perforations in the face bones of this Timucua skull. For more forensic anthropology, see Chapter 9.

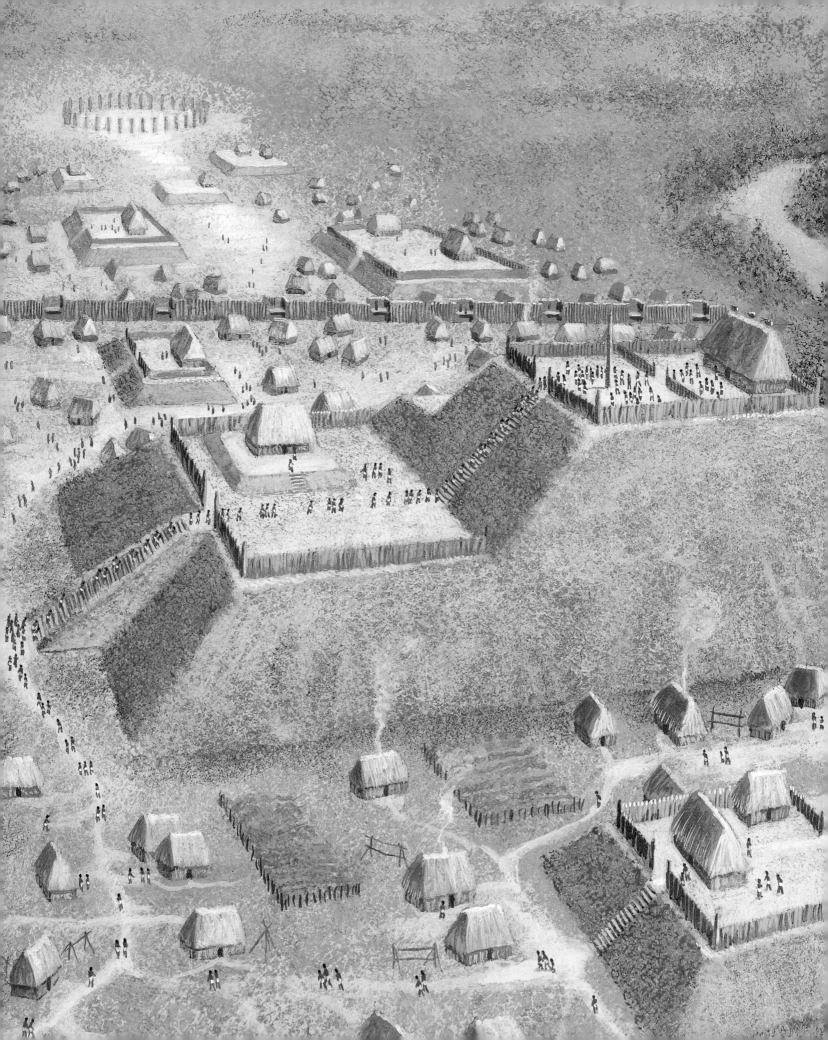

Metropolis on the Mississippi

French explorers Marquette and Jolliet sailed right by it in 1673 and never knew it was there.

So did American explorers Lewis and Clark in 1804, though they did write in their journals that they found some Indian mounds, lots of broken pottery, and pieces of flint on the shoreline where the Mississippi and Missouri Rivers converge. But how could they miss it? It's as tall as a ten-story building, and it covers 14 acres (that's bigger than a dozen soccer fields!). What they missed was the biggest pyramid in the United States and Canada.

One reason why the early explorers failed to recognize Monks Mound is that it is made of earth. It doesn't have any stone facing like Egypt's pyramids, and it isn't stuccoed over and painted in bright colors like the Mexican pyramids, so it's easy to mistake for a natural hill. Monks Mound got its name from a group of French monks who had built a monastery on the banks of Cahokia Creek, which ran by it. But when President Thomas Jefferson's good friend Henry Brackenridge arrived in the area in 1811, he knew what he was looking for. St. Louis wasn't called the Mound City for nothing. Brackenridge had heard that there were many Indian mounds on the edge of the Mississippi/Missouri floodplain, or bottomlands.

A thousand years ago, Cahokia was North America's biggest city.

The builders of St. Louis weren't the first people to realize that the intersection of two of America's great rivers wouldn't be a bad place to build a city. The location offered great soil for planting and a watery highway to sail and trade on.

Hacking his way through the cedar- and willow-covered bluffs, Brackenridge noticed that the mounds got bigger and bigger—and that they were regularly spaced. He felt he was being deliberately led to some important place. Suddenly he found himself standing in front of "a stupendous pile of earth." Awestruck, he would later write to the president: "I was astonished that this

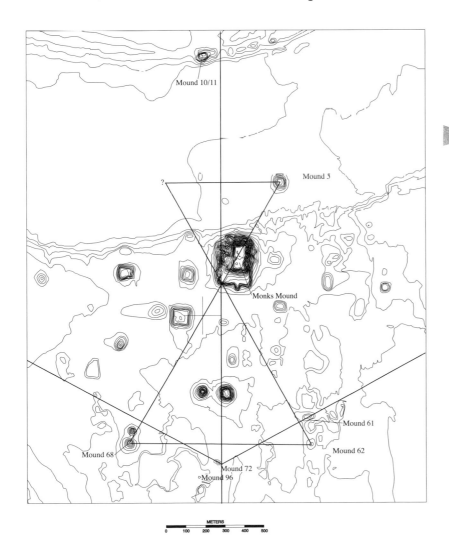

Cahokia's plan is very orderly. One-hundred-foot-high Monks Mound (middle) is surrounded by four plazas, one for each of the cardinal directions of the universe: north, south, east, and west. The central axis of the city divides it into two parts that seem to mirror each other. Mound 72 lies at the opposite end of the north–south axis, just outside the fortified area. Can you identify the mounds in the model on the previous page?

stupendous monument of antiquity should have been unnoticed by any traveler." Monks Mound is the biggest of 120 mounds at Cahokia. Its 22 million cubic feet of earth were carried by hand in baskets in 50-pound loads. That's 15 million basketloads! "We can scarcely bring ourselves to believe it was built without other means of collecting and conveying material than that possessed by the Indians," an early archaeologist would write. But then we seem to have a long history of underestimating the skills of the first North Americans.

Monks Mound is far too large to excavate fully, but soil core samples (see page 115 for similar procedure) show it was built in stages between 900 and 1200 CE. Trenching (see page 97) reveals that a wooden building 104 by 48 feet once stood on top. This must have been the chief's house. Traces of his dishes and pots were found in an eating area. Some of his treasures were dug up, too: copper bells, decorated pots, and a stone tablet with a carving of a birdman. Who knows how many earlier chiefs lie buried beneath it?

Now, let's turn back the clock a thousand years and stand where Brackenridge stood. Imagine Monks Mound in 1000 CE. It supports a huge pole-and-thatch temple, the residence of an elite class of rulers. The great pyramid has a 200-acre plaza in front of it, and it's surrounded by a stockade made out of 20,000 twelve-foot-long logs. That alone would have taken a crew of one hundred workers twenty years working eight hours a day to accomplish—without a day off! The grass roof of the temple on top of Monks Mound is decorated with wood carvings of animals covered with feathers.

We're here for the biggest holiday of the year—it happens in mid-July. Fifteen thousand residents are crowded into the plaza around us. They have come from near and far to celebrate the Green Corn festival. Other outsiders are here for the ceremony, too. There's a group of traders carrying baskets of chert stone from distant quarries to exchange for local products, such as salt and bear teeth. Merchants who have arrived in the market earlier argue and barter to get the best prices for their pearls, shells, arrowheads, fancy digging sticks, pots, copper jewelry, and foods like pumpkins, herbs, and fish. When the sun stands highest in the sky, the chief emerges from the temple. He is dressed in a feather robe and headdress. From his neck hangs a heavy shell necklace with a conch-shell pendant carved with the image of Eagle Man—his spirit guide. The chief makes an offering to the gods and announces that the corn is ripe. Let the harvest begin!

A long procession of representatives from lesser cities lines up to pay tribute to the chief. They offer him gifts of copper, shells, polished chunks of obsidian, lead, and mica. The celebration goes on late into the night as pine torches around the stockade light the plaza. People play games, and the air is filled with sweet-smelling smoke from

Flanked by his attendants, the great chief of Cahokia greets the rising sun on the day of the Green Corn festival.

the cooking stalls. We all go home exhausted!

This was Cahokia—the biggest of all the Mississippian, or Temple Mound, sites built on the banks of the Mississippi River, stretching from Illinois to Louisiana between 500 and 1200 CE. Some people think the site is laid out in the shape of a giant sacred bird. Have a look at the map on page 91 and see what you think. At its height, Cahokia had a population of 15,000 people.

These beautiful artifacts were all discovered at Cahokia. They include many different points and a tablet with a drawing of Bearded Birdman on it (see page 100).

The Mississippian culture that built Cahokia followed and even overlapped with the less advanced Adena and Hopewell, whom we met earlier. Mississippians made two kinds of pottery: utilitarian (for the household) and ceremonial (decorated, usually for burials or gifts to honor an important person). Both were made in many different styles. Mississippians had lots of technological artifacts, too: hoes made out of stone, shell, and the shoulder bones of large animals; shell cups and bowls; copper and bone fishhooks; drills; knives; scrapers; and grinding stones to process corn. The pottery and exotic items were lavish.

As we have seen, Cahokia's pyramids were huge, and the spaces around them were elaborate and well organized. To create the pyramids and the exotic items archaeologists have found inside them required an advanced degree of organization. This is why Cahokia is regarded as a state by archaeologists.

Stairway leading up to Monks Mound. North America's largest pyramid has a base that covers about 14 acres. That's as large as ten and a half football fields!

Archaeology tells the story of who built Cahokia. "In excavating near the base of the great temple mount of Cahokia," wrote a nineteenth-century archaeologist, "we found in a crumbling tomb of earth and stone a great number [more than 100] of burial vases... some of these were painted and there were also the paint-pots and dishes holding the colors." Since then, archaeologists have pulled thousands of objects out of the ground beneath the ancient city.

It's the mid-1970s and the archaeologists are busily excavating Mound 72, just outside the southern boundary of "downtown" Cahokia. You can scarcely find Mound 72 on a map, but it will turn out to be one of the city's most important mounds. What lies inside it tells us that the Cahokia people once had an elaborate death cult—a specialized set of religious rituals to honor the dead.

Mound 72 is one of the more unusual of Cahokia's 120 mounds. Find it on the map on page 91. First, it's rectangular, measuring 140 by 70 feet. Second, it's the only mound that has a ridge on top. Third, it's twisted out of line from all the other mounds so that it points to where the sun sets on the first day of summer. It could have been used as a sun-worshipping station or perhaps to keep track of the seasons of the year. Maybe the Mississippians deposited materials there that they used in their rituals. *This mound would be a great place to excavate!* thought archaeologist Melvin Fowler.

Archaeologists usually begin an excavation by stringing together a grid of 1-meter squares so they can record exactly where in *space* they find an artifact. (You can see some examples of grids on pages 100 and 102.) As they dig down into each square of the grid, they record the *depth* where they find each item. Knowing the depth is important because the deeper you dig, the farther back you go in history.

As the archaeologists are making their map, Fowler notices still another curiosity about Mound 72. One edge of it lines up exactly north–south with a corner of Monks Mound and the edge of another mound (10/11) half a mile farther north. Also, two other mounds (62 and 68) lie at equal distances from the north–south line. He wonders: Could it be that the whole city was planned by people (like Ohio's Hopewell) who understood and prized geometry, angles, and

▶ Dr. Melvin Fowler surveying the remains of Cahokia.

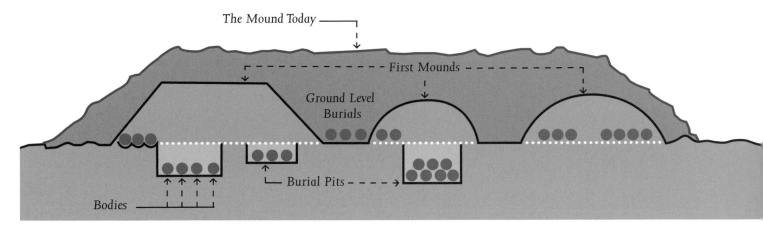

The Mound Today

First Mounds

Ground Level
Burials

Burial Pits

Bodies

How does this cross section of a Cahokia mound show changes in its shape over time?

measuring units? Fowler had heard of a large post used to mark the exact center of another site. Maybe Mound 72 was a deliberately placed "marker mound." Now he has a hypothesis he can test. He tells his student workers: "Put a trench in right here," as he points to a square on the grid map. "I bet we'll find a big post pit there."

Archaeologists dig test trenches: They make straight sided narrow cuts into the sides of pyramids, which is a process called trenching. They can discover part of a wall, a storage place, or, if they're lucky, a section of a tomb. Fowler hopes, in this case, for a post pit. The workers probe the mosquito- and poison ivy-infested turf carefully with their mattocks—straight-sided, flat-bottomed shovels. Down they go: 1 meter, 2—nothing. Then Fowler realizes he has miscalculated. "Wait! Move it three meters south and start over," he commands. Sure enough, at a 1-meter depth they hit pay dirt, a dark stain on the ground in the shape of a circle—a post pit! The people who built Cahokia *did* have a plan. They were more sophisticated than most archaeologists had thought. As the students dig further into the past—all the way down to 3 meters (9 feet)—they learn that three different posts had occupied that space. At the bottom of the pit, they find the remains of the corner of a small log building. They carefully collect the fragments and send them back to the lab for

WOODHENGE: THE "BIG BEN" OF CAHOKIA

Like all great cities, Cahokia has a giant clock. It is called Woodhenge and is a circle of forty-eight posts 400 feet in diameter. That's it at the extreme left of the panoramic view on page 90. There is no evidence that Woodhenge was ever covered over, so we know it couldn't have been a shelter or a residence. There's a post hole placed off center that gives just the right angles to fit the key dates when the sun appears over each post, when viewed from that point. Archaeologists believe Cahokia priests used Woodhenge as a giant sun calendar to mark important dates of the year, like the solstices and the equinoxes. The rising sun at the equinox would line up with the off-center post. Minutes before, it appeared at the post in the background. Keeping track of the schedule of religious worship is very important in highly organized state societies.

The rising sun on the first day of autumn is about to appear over one of Woodhenge's posts. Why would the Cahokia state need an accurate calendar?

radiocarbon dating. A few weeks later, the date comes back: 940 CE. Clearly, Mound 72 is very old, and since it was marked by a big post, it must have been very important. But what else lies inside? Fowler orders trenches dug on the other side.

If you think you can learn all there is about the life of an archaeologist by watching an Indiana Jones movie, guess again! Professor Fowler's students are dedicated workers. Like most archaeologists, they've wanted to dig and explore since they were kids. And like most archaeologists, they spend much of their time sweating in the hot sun, getting eaten by bugs, digging through thick, greasy clay and mud, filtering soil through screens so they don't lose even a tiny artifact—and usually not finding a whole lot. Then there's the rain that fills the pits they've excavated. It leaves behind a frothy black puddle with ancient bone fragments floating on it. The water in the pits has to be pumped out and the mucky bottom sopped up with sponges before the dig can resume. The next day, the blazing sun can dry out the bottom of the pit into a layer as hard as concrete. Yes, archaeology is hard work—but you do it because you're excited to discover the past.

On this day, in Cahokia's Mound 72, the results will make it all worthwhile. At a 1-meter depth, one of the worker's shovels makes a crunching sound. It's the top of a huge pile of white projectile points—a cache, or offering, deliberately placed in that location. Now it's time to get out the dental picks and fine brushes for some close-up precision work. It will take days to carefully clear and remove more than 800 points. At 1½ meters, just under the points, the workers find another white object that is much larger. It's a bone—but so fragile a bone that, when one of the students uses his pick to remove the surrounding soil, it crumbles to dust. Workers try to stabilize the bone first with glue and then by pouring hot wax over fabric to cover it so it

Judging from the decorations buried with him, Bearded Birdman must have been a very important leader in Cahokia.

can hold its shape.

That bone is the right thighbone of the "Bearded Birdman," a forty-year-old human male who had been buried in a shower of valuable objects. He is resting on a bed of 20,000 shells in the shape of a falcon. Piled in several huge heaps around him are 800 unused arrowheads, strange stone disks called chunkey stones, sheets of mica carved in intricate shapes, and a 3-foot-long roll of copper sheeting. Birdman is just one of 280 people buried in Mound 72. It will take four years for Fowler and his team to carefully dig all of them up. Fowler discovers four men who have no heads or hands among the occupants of Mound 72. Forensic anthropologists who later examine their bones discover straight, sharp cuts across the neck vertebrae at the base of the

After removing Bearded Birdman from his elaborate grave, Cahokia archaeologists excavated this cache of projectile points.

skull. They had been decapitated! The archaeologists excavate four mass graves in Mound 72—graves that contain only young women between the ages of fifteen and twenty-five. In one of the graves, students count fifty women lined up in rows and stacked three deep. Dental experts discover that these women came from different gene pools—they couldn't all have been citizens of Cahokia. Other graves in Mound 72 are found to hold people of high status. Prior to burial, they had been carefully wrapped in blankets and carried there on litters—beds made out of thatch. Other people buried there seem to be of lower status. Judging from the way they appear, it seems that these victims must have been lined up at the edge of the pit, then struck from behind with a blunt instrument such as a stone axe. They either fell into the pit or they were pushed. Some of these victims' fingers were found clawing at the sand up the side of the pit as if they were trying to climb out. They weren't

PLAYING CHUNKEY

A chunkey stone is a highly polished disk about the size of an adult's hand. Mississippians used them to play a game. You take turns rolling chunkey stones down a long court. Other players throw long spears at the place where they think the stone will stop. Whoever comes closest gets a point.

A carved, polished chunkey stone from Cahokia. What sports could you compare with the game of chunkey?

How many different kinds of artifacts can you identify in Bearded Birdman's grave?

dead when they were buried! Some burials were reburials—people already dead many years, dug up and moved to Mound 72.

Mound 72 turns out to be a buildup of more than a century of burials in three mounds that were eventually joined together. The post pits marked the special places where the dead would be sent off to the afterworld. The small log building at the bottom was a charnel house, where the bodies were stored. It was dismantled, and the earliest reburials were placed in a mound on top of it. On top of that came the young women, the headless men, and finally Bearded Birdman. But who were these people? Why would members of an advanced civilization like Cahokia have executed some of them so brutally, while treating other dead people with great reverence? And why did the Cahokians develop the death cult whose remains we find in Mound 72? To answer these questions, let me first ask you some questions about yourself and how you relate to other members of society—questions that might seem, at least at first, to have nothing to do with ancient burials.

Who's your friend? How will you keep his or her loyalty over time? How do you know your friend won't find a better friend to bond with? Now, just imagine trying to maintain loyalty and friendship in complex societies along the Mississippi River a thousand years ago. Controlling the waterway and keeping 15,000 people happy and content—proud to be Cahokian—would have been very important for survival. In Cahokia, as in the land of the Tlingit and Haida of the Northwest Coast, you bonded with friends by displaying your unique goods to the people and to the gods at public functions. Funerary rites were Cahokia's most important function. Goods—and people—from faraway places were put into Mound 72 to show future generations that their ancestors were great and powerful. It validates and records how far back Cahokia power goes because it contains the reburied bones of early ancestors alongside the body of the current ruler.

We don't know what kinds of rituals accompanied Cahokia funerals, but studying historical records of later Mississippian people can give us some clues. At the Fatherland site, more than 1,000 miles down the Mississippi River from Cahokia, we know that, at the time of contact with the first

A model of the kind of thatched hut common in Cahokia.

Europeans, approximately 500 years after the abandonment of Cahokia, a French explorer described one gruesome ceremony: Women were lined up and each was given a plug of tobacco to chew to dull her senses. They were then all strangled from behind and pushed into their graves. The Natchez Indian rulers, likely Cahokia descendants, conducted sacrifices of their slaves. It may come as a surprise to us, but some slaves proudly volunteered to accompany their leader into the afterworld as a way of demonstrating their own high status and great loyalty to their family.

One of the great lessons archaeologists learn from the study of ancient cities is that no civilization's power can last forever. The top layers of Mound 72 tell the end of the story of Cahokia. These layers don't have a lot of exotic goods, and the caches are smaller. Evidently Cahokia was no longer a wealthy and prosperous city. It was beginning to fall into decay. Remember from our discussion of the Anasazi: We already know that the early thirteenth century was a time of drought in much of what we now call the United States. The scarcity of natural resources probably led to unrest and maybe war among competing Mississippian towns. Their bones tell us that these later people also may have developed health problems from an unbalanced diet that was beginning to become too heavily based on corn. All of these factors led to a gradual breakup of the great city. As the population decreased, those who left probably blended into smaller towns located on higher land more distant from the bottomlands of the river. By the fourteenth century, only six generations before the first explorers would arrive, Mound 72, Monks Mound, and all the other mounds that once made up North America's first true city were already overgrown—so overgrown that Lewis and Clark, and Marquette and Jolliet, wouldn't have had a chance of finding the lost city.

9 • THE SCIENTISTS

Time Detectives... and the Clues They Use

Putting together a time puzzle is a lot like solving a crime. First, you need to gather all the parts of the puzzle—the evidence—and then piece them together. Many people specialize in solving the puzzles of the peopling of the Americas. They ask who were the first North Americans? Where did they come from? When did they get here? How did they change as they tried to adapt to different environments? We have already met the archaeologists who are part of the team of puzzle solvers. But biologists (they study the structure of cells), physical anthropologists (they study bones and teeth), linguists (they study languages), and forensic anthropologists (they put together human forms from bone fragments) also contribute to answering these questions.

BIOLOGISTS

The story of who you are and where you came from is encoded in your cells. Your history lives in your genes and in the molecules in your body that make up those genes. Genes mutate: They change as succeeding generations try to cope with changes that take place in their environment. Blood types change, too. So do the antibodies in our blood as they try to set up new game plans to defend our bodies against strange new diseases that might invade them. Cell biologists identify genetic markers, which they can use to measure how distant a relative you are from someone else. The closer these markers are between two groups of people, the closer the group's ancestry.

Molecular biologists can single out our relatives very accurately by studying mitochondrial DNA (MtDNA). It's a large molecule found in our mitochondria, tiny portions of cells that help make energy out of the food we eat. Biologists use MtDNA as a clock. Here's the key: All children get MtDNA from their mothers. Because Dad's genes don't contribute to MtDNA, changes in MtDNA from generation to generation are fairly easy to follow. This molecule changes in structure, or mutates, very fast, which means you can use it as an accurate measure of generations over time. The greater the number of generations, the more changes occur.

To accomplish this, scientists start by choosing two test groups of people that they know split off from each other. For example, they might collect DNA samples from living descendants of Pilgrims who came over to America on the *Mayflower* and compare their DNA with samples taken from their relatives who remained in England. When they measure how much the MtDNA molecule has mutated in the time since the two groups separated, they can calibrate, or adjust, the scale of the MtDNA clock so that they can tell how far

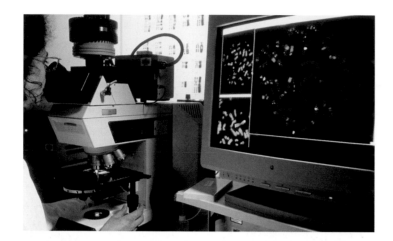

Biologists use a high-power electron microscope like this one (top) to examine the structure of DNA (bottom).

apart in ancestry any pair of groups of people might be. The next step would be to collect DNA samples from people who live today on both sides of the Bering Strait and calculate how long ago their common ancestors separated from one another when some of them walked across the ancient land bridge and others stayed behind. Result: The differences in the samples show that these groups split up sometime between 20,000 and 56,000 years ago. A more recent study of changes in Y chromosomes—another part of the DNA molecule that boys inherit only from their fathers—gives dates closer to 18,000 years.

PHYSICAL ANTHROPOLOGISTS

Using human remains larger than cells is another way to figure out when the Beringian migration took place. Did you "inherit" your mom's or your dad's teeth? Because they outlast our body's soft parts and bones, and because they change slowly from generation to generation, teeth can be used by physical anthropologists to trace family lineages. There are many characteristics of teeth (size, shape, etc.) that are hereditary, or passed on from parents to their children. How many roots are on your first molar? What does the cusp on your second molar look like? Are your incisors (pointy teeth) shovel- or spatula-shaped? By studying the changes in 200,000 teeth from 9,000 different remains of ancient people found at archaeological sites, physical anthropologists have calculated a "splitting-off" time of 13,500 years of the first Americans from people who remained in Asia. If you compare this result with what we learned from MtDNA, you'll see that not all parts of the puzzle fit together perfectly!

LINGUISTS

The words we use provide clues to where we came from—and when. When I was a kid growing up in New England, I'd order a *soda* and ask the clerk to put it in a *bag*.

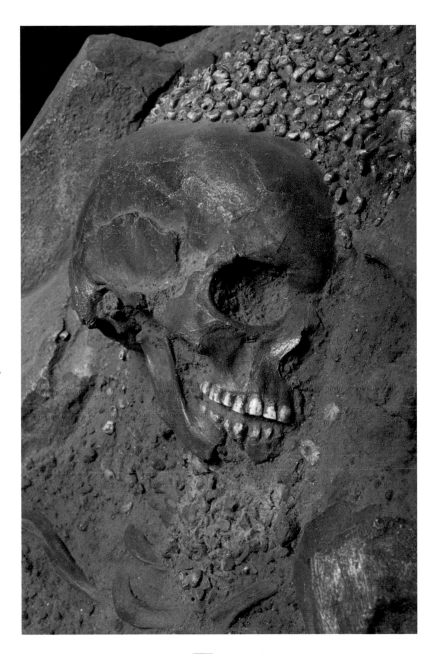

By examining the shape of the teeth on a specimen like this one, physical anthropologists can tell who its ancestors were.

Can you think of other place names that come from Native American words?

When I later moved to Arizona, I learned that I had better ask for a *pop* and have it put in a *sack*. Word differences like these, and the accents that go with them (everybody knows Texans sound different from Minnesotans), develop among groups who get out of contact with one another. I remember visiting my cousins a few years after they moved south from Connecticut to Florida and thinking they "talked funny."

Linguists study what words came through those ancient teeth that the physical anthropologists study to trace family connections. Today's American Indians speak close to 1,000 languages. Back when people lived in small extended and isolated families, they developed their own words, expressions, slang, and accents. Tribes living 100 miles apart probably couldn't converse with one another.

Linguists collect shared-word lists from native groups. They arrange them in "word families" based on the relative number of words they share. It's the same story as MtDNA and teeth: The closer the word families, the more recent

the splitting off time. And the greater the difference, the more widespread we'd expect to find them in space. For example, Amerind, a collection of North American word families that covers most of North and all of South America, shares 281 words. All of them use the sound n to address the first person. (Europeans use m, as in me, in English, or moi, in French.) One conclusion based on the languages the various Native American descendants of the ancient Beringians now speak is that a major Siberian crossing can't be much later than 14,500 years ago.

As you can see, scientists use many methods for determining when the great migration began; some of them more precise than others. All the dating seems to converge on a time roughly 20,000 years ago, although all scientists must remain open to new information that might change their estimates.

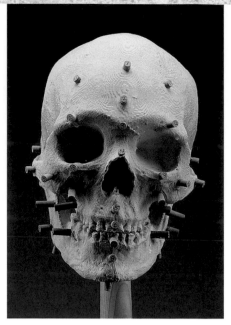

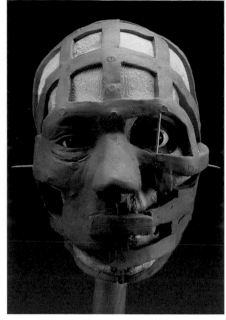

1   2   3

FORENSIC ANTHROPOLOGISTS

Finding an undamaged skull at an archaeological site is pretty rare. However, by piecing together fragments and comparing measurements, forensic anthropologists can determine the age and gender of an individual. They can also tell members of one tribe from another. This knowledge helps trace how people moved and mixed after the Beringian migration.

This is an example of how a skull is reconstructed. Sharon Long, a forensic sculptress and anthropologist in Wyoming, made this reconstruction from the skull of a modern human, Sergeant Charles Floyd, who was the only person to die on the Lewis and Clark expedition.

1. First, she makes a mold and plaster cast of the original skull and adds tissue thickness depth markers to the cast.

2. She connects the markers methodically with plastina clay strips and then fills in the spaces by adding more clay strips.

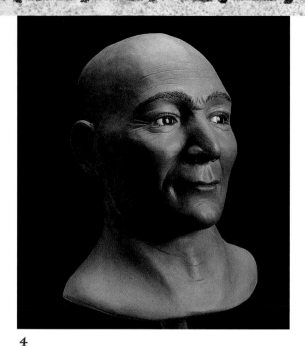

4

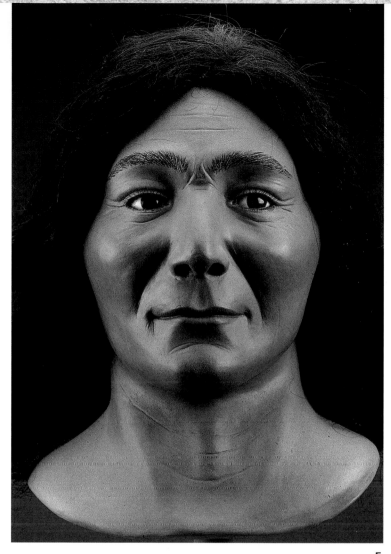

5

3. Then, like a sculptor, she builds up the face by blocking in the mouth and nose, setting in glass eyes, and forming its features.

4. Next, she adds age markings according to information from physical anthropologists who determined how old the person's bones were when he or she died.

5. Finally, she makes a mold and plaster cast of the completed facial reconstruction. A little smoothing and shiny finish and a wig of human hair give a likely face to match an old skull.

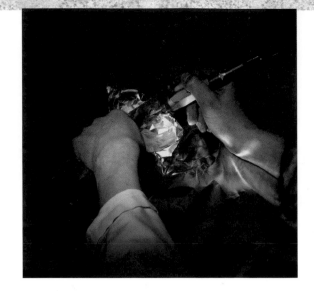

A scientist scrapes shavings from a reindeer bone to find out how old it is.

RADIOCARBON DATING

Have you ever noticed when you check out the refrigerator for leftovers that the longer something's been in there, the older it looks and, if it has been in there long enough, the worse it smells? That's because it decays. Archaeologists use a decay principle called radiocarbon dating to measure the age of any material that was once alive—for example, a wooden mummy case that once was a tree or the charred remains from a fire of some ancient person's dinner.

Trees grow in vast reservoirs of air. Carbon dioxide is among the gases they take in. The carbon in the carbon dioxide molecules is made up mostly of stable carbon (called C12). But it also has a tiny portion of radioactive carbon (C14). Radioactive carbon decays, or changes into C12, with a half-life of 5,730 years. That means if you start out with 1 ounce of a fifty-fifty mixture of C12 and C14, after 5,730 years, you'll be left with half of the radioactive sample, or ¾ ounce of C12 and ¼ ounce of C14. The ratio of C12 to C14 would be 3 to 1. After 2 × 5,730 years, or 11,460 years, half of the ¼ ounce of C14 will have decayed. You will then have a C12-to-C14 ratio of 7 to 1 (⅞ ounce of C12 to ⅛ ounce of C14). The greater the time span, the lower the ratio.

Today	C12	C14
5,730 years from now	C12	C14
11,460 years from now	C12	C14

As long as a tree remains alive, it keeps exchanging carbon dioxide with the atmosphere, so the C12-to-C14 ratio doesn't change. Now, suppose Egyptian priests order a tree cut down to make a case to hold a king's mummy. As soon as the tree stops breathing, its C12-to-C14 ratio will start to decrease. Archaeologists who excavate the mummy can measure the ratio and compare it with the C12-to-C14 ratio in the atmosphere. That's how they "date" the wood in the coffin and what's inside. But beware! The radiocarbon method isn't 100 percent reliable. First, there's no way to be sure that today's C12-to-C14 ratio in the Earth's atmosphere is the same as it was then. Second, what if the wood had been reused? Then the mummy's case wouldn't be as old as the radiocarbon date would indicate. Finally, archaeologists need to be very careful when collecting samples for radiocarbon dating because of contamination by surrounding deposits of different ages. So, pinning down the earliest date for people arriving on this continent isn't as certain as scientists would like it to be.

ICE CORES AND A GLACIER'S TIME MACHINE

In the middle of Greenland the snow never melts. It just accumulates in layers that get more and more compressed as time passes. It forms huge glaciers, known as ice sheets. The history of the world lies encased in these ice sheets. Air bubbles, dust pollen, and microorganisms blown by the winds get trapped in the fallen snow. Half a mile below the glacier's surface are lead particles from ancient Roman metal processing furnaces; at 1 mile deep the air trapped in the ice is the same as that breathed by the first cave dwellers. At the very bottom of the glacier lie the compact remains of the first snowfall that

This ice coring operation shows the core being carefully pulled from the drill.

began the last ice age more than 100,000 years ago.

In the 1990s glaciologists drilled straight down through 2 miles of the Greenland ice sheet. They used a hollow pipe with teeth on the outside. As the teeth chipped deeper through the ice, a core sample went into the pipe. Scientists carefully wrapped the core in sections and put them in Styrofoam boxes to be flown in unheated planes to laboratories in Denver, Colorado, and Copenhagen, Denmark, where the samples were placed in freezers. Experts who "read" the frozen history book learned that a great worldwide melting took place about 20,000 years ago. Previously ice had covered one-third of our planet and much of North America as far south as New York City. It was during this great melting that the southern part of the land bridge that once connected Asia and Alaska became exposed. That's when the great human migration into our once-empty American continent began.

DATES FROM STUDYING TREE RINGS

Imagine growing a new skin every year! Clams, coral, and most trees add one layer a year to their outer structures. Check out any cross section of a tree and you can see its growth bands. At the sawed-off end of a tree log, the bands look like rings. If you count the rings, you'll discover how old the tree was when it was cut down. If you know when the tree was cut, you'll be able to connect each ring with a specific year. Archaeologists call this absolute dating because, like radiocarbon, it gives you a real date.

The thicker a tree's ring, the better the growing season. Dendrochronologists collect tree ring records from many different samples—an old log cabin, a dead tree lying in the forest, the support posts from an ancient pit house or kiva, even cores taken from long-living trees that still thrive. They look for patterns and sequences that can be identified in the different samples. By matching overlapping patterns, they can trace the relative dates farther and farther back in time. If they know the absolute date of a recent sample—say, the living tree—then scientists can get the absolute date of any wooden artifact in which they can detect the same tree ring pattern. This gives the date the tree was cut down. But just as in radiocarbon dating, there are problems. For example, how do you know your date is the same date when the wood was used—or reused—in an artifact?

Drilling cores in trees is similar to drilling cores in a glacier. Here a dendrochronologist looks at the core record (top). Each ring of the tree represents a season of growth (bottom). Check it out next time you run across a fallen tree or branch.

AUTHOR'S NOTE

I am never more excited than when I take my students to the ancient ruins left behind by the first Americans. Whether we walk on the back of an earth serpent in Ohio, stand on the edge of the mesa in Chaco Canyon, climb the steps to the top of Monks Mound, or enter the tomb of a Maya king in the rain forests of Central America—nothing can surpass the experience of seeing things for ourselves. I remember our first visit to Palenque, the ancient Maya ruins buried deep in the jungle of southeastern Mexico, to see the tomb of the ruler Pacal. We climbed down sixty slimy steps accessed from a trapdoor at the top of a pyramid. Then we entered the chamber of a dead king that had been sealed for more than a thousand years. There he lay, jade face mask intact, showered with obsidian and shell jewelry—unmoved since his subjects first laid him there. What an important person he must have been in his day!

In our field studies, my students and I measure and map ruins with surveying equipment. We're especially interested in the way ancient astronomers and architects aligned their pyramids with celestial bodies that represented the gods they worshipped. I study fragments of ancient documents to decipher the numbers, words, and pictures that tell why they aligned buildings and temples as they did.

Though I originally studied astronomy, my interest in people later made me into an anthropologist as well. I try to reflect my combined interests in what I write. Some of my other books include *Empires of Time: Calendars, Clocks, and Cultures* (University Press of Colorado, 2002). There I explore why clocks and calendars were invented. *Conversing with the Planets: How Science and Myth Invented the Cosmos* (University Press of Colorado, 2002) explores what the universe means to us and what it meant to our ancestors. *Stairways to the Stars: Skywatching in Three Great Ancient Cultures* (Wiley, 1997) is about archaeoastronomy, the study of how people in different cultures acquired knowledge from the sky. *Ancient Astronomers* (Smithsonian, 1993) is an easily readable book for teens that tells why people all over the world—from China to Polynesia to ancient America—have been fascinated by the sky and how their knowledge of the constellation patterns and the movements of the planets changed their cultures. Magic fascinates me, too. In *Behind the Crystal Ball: Magic, Science, and the Occult from Antiquity Through the New Age* (University Press of Colorado, 2002), I take readers on a tour through time and space as I try to unveil the many ways people have used magic over the millennia in hopes of improving their lives.

Studying cultures other than our own is a lot like looking in a mirror. Learning about *them* is a great way to learn about *ourselves*. To think that Mexico's Aztec, Peru's Inca, and Ohio's Hopewell all came from a great journey undertaken long ago by simple bands of hunter-gatherers who were fortunate and strong enough to survive the harsh climate of Siberia and Alaska is almost too much for me to believe. But the evidence is there to prove that it really happened. I hope your journey with me through the pages of *The First Americans* has excited you as much as it has thrilled me to take you to these new and fascinating places. But don't take my word for it—go and see some of the evidence for yourself!

WHERE TO GO TO DISCOVER
THE FIRST NORTH AMERICANS

It's a good bet that wherever you live, there's an archaeological site nearby. Most of the North American sites you've read about in this book are pretty easy to get to. Let me get you started with a brief list of my favorite national and state parks, where some of these sites are located:

Aztec National Monument, New Mexico

Gila Cliff Dwellings National Monument, New Mexico

Mesa Verde National Park, Colorado

Cahokia Mounds State Historic Site, Illinois

Fort Ancient, Ohio

Fatherland Site, Natchez, Mississippi

Poverty Point State Park, Epps, Louisiana

Newark Mounds, Newark, Ohio

Crystal River State Park, Crystal River, Florida

Moundsville State Park, Moundsville, Alabama

Etowah State Park, Indian Mounds Historic Site, Cartersville, Georgia

If you want to follow descendants of the great migration who moved farther south than those we've discussed, you need to travel south of our borders. Mexican archaeological sites are also relatively easy to get to. If you start in Cancún, Mexico, you can easily visit Maya ruins like Chichén Itzá, Cobá, and Tulum in a day or two. There are good family hotels to stay at nearby. If you start in Mexico City, you can see Aztec Tenochtítlan's Great Temple and the nearby colossal pyramids of ancient Teotihuacán. Don't miss the National Museum of Anthropology while you're there. Visiting these places will help you to better understand that all of the native populations of the Americas—both north *and* south—are one people. For group tours to any of these places consult *Archaeology Magazine* or *Dig*, an archaeology magazine for kids.

Museums in many major American cities house collections of artifacts and offer exhibitions that show how the first North Americans lived. Here's a short list of my favorite museums:

National Museum of American History, Washington, D.C.

National Museum of the American Indian, Washington, D.C.

Alaska Museum of Natural History, Anchorage, Alaska

Arizona Historical Society, Tucson, Arizona

California Indian Museum and Cultural Center, Santa Rosa, California

Anasazi Heritage Center, Dolores, Colorado

Museo de las Américas, Denver, Colorado

Nashantucket Pequot Muscum, Nashantucket, Connecticut

Peabody Museum of Archaeology and Ethnology, Harvard University, Cambridge, Massachusetts

Museum of Anthropology at the University of Michigan, Ann Arbor, Michigan

Maxwell Anthropology Museum at the University of New Mexico, Albuquerque, New Mexico

Seneca-Iroquois National Museum, Salamanca, New York

Museum of the Cherokee Indian, Cherokee, North Carolina

Haffenreffer Museum of Anthropology, Brown University, Providence, Rhode Island

Makah Cultural and Research Center, Neah Bay, Washington

Canadian Museum of Civilization, Gatineau, Quebec, Canada

Museum of Archaeology and Ethnology, Burnaby Mountain, British
Columbia, Canada

Royal Ontario Museum, Toronto, Ontario, Canada

University of Pennsylvania Museum of Archaeology and Anthropology,
Philadelphia, Pennsylvania

The Web can help you locate Native American museums and archaeological sites near you—or plan a vacation/visit to one farther away that might interest you. Three of my favorite museum Web sites are

www.museumstuff.com

www.hanksville.org/NAresources/indices/NAMuseums.html
(gives a state-by-state listing)

www.multcolib.org/homework/natamhc.html
(lists official national Web sites and much more)

Now that you're equipped with the basic knowledge, you can explore the first North Americans you're most curious about on your own!

PHOTO CREDITS

INDEX

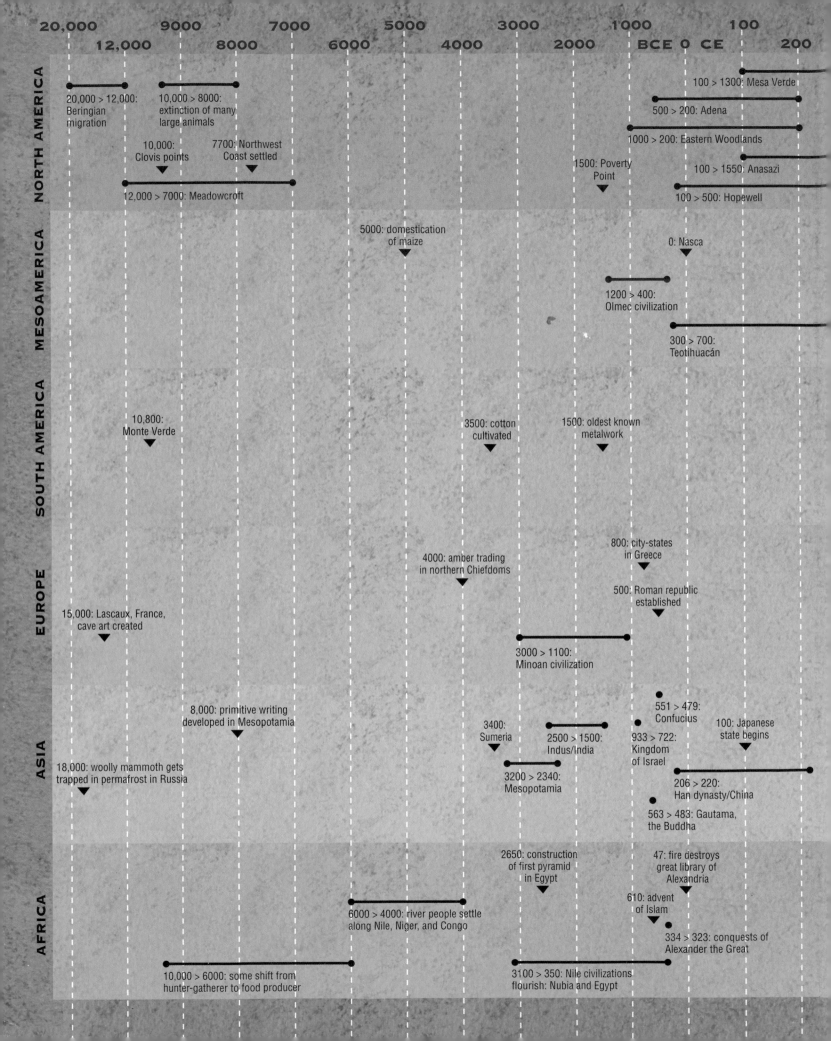

20,000   **9000**   **7000**   **5000**   **3000**   **1000**   **100**

12,000   **8000**   **6000**   **4000**   **2000**   **BCE 0 CE**   **200**

NORTH AMERICA

20,000 > 12,000: Beringian migration

10,000 > 8000: extinction of many large animals

10,000: Clovis points

7700: Northwest Coast settled

12,000 > 7000: Meadowcroft

100 > 1300: Mesa Verde

500 > 200: Adena

1000 > 200: Eastern Woodlands

1500: Poverty Point

100 > 1550: Anasazi

100 > 500: Hopewell

MESOAMERICA

5000: domestication of maize

0: Nasca

1200 > 400: Olmec civilization

300 > 700: Teotihuacán

SOUTH AMERICA

10,800: Monte Verde

3500: cotton cultivated

1500: oldest known metalwork

EUROPE

800: city-states in Greece

4000: amber trading in northern Chiefdoms

500: Roman republic established

15,000: Lascaux, France, cave art created

3000 > 1100: Minoan civilization

ASIA

551 > 479: Confucius

8,000: primitive writing developed in Mesopotamia

100: Japanese state begins

3400: Sumeria

2500 > 1500: Indus/India

933 > 722: Kingdom of Israel

18,000: woolly mammoth gets trapped in permafrost in Russia

3200 > 2340: Mesopotamia

206 > 220: Han dynasty/China

563 > 483: Gautama, the Buddha

AFRICA

2650: construction of first pyramid in Egypt

47: fire destroys great library of Alexandria

610: advent of Islam

6000 > 4000: river people settle along Nile, Niger, and Congo

334 > 323: conquests of Alexander the Great

10,000 > 6000: some shift from hunter-gatherer to food producer

3100 > 350: Nile civilizations flourish: Nubia and Egypt